RICHMOND PARISH CHURCH

A Doctor's Christianity

W H Tattersall

A Doctor's Christianity

BY

W H Tattersall

New Millennium
310 Kennington Road London SE11 4LD

Printed & bound by BWD Ltd. Northolt, Middx.
Typeset in 12pt Gatineau
Issued by New Millennium*
ISBN 1 85845 005 5

*An imprint of The Professional Authors' & Publishers' Association

Dedication

To Joan Novello,
our children,
and our nine grand children

Contents

PAGE

Foreword

By the Rev., the Lord Soper, M.A., Ph.D., D.D.

I am glad to have the opportunity of commending *A Doctor's Christianity* and for a number of clear reasons. It is written by a doctor, so was the Gospel of St. Luke, and never was the relationship between the vocation of healing and the proclamation of the gospel so greatly needed. The author establishes a clear and unbroken relationship between the ministry of healing and the ministry of the word.

Then again, it is not extravagant to say that this book is in the great tradition (of which Pascal, the Frenchman, is perhaps the greatest exponent) of claiming the place of reason in every aspect of belief. Once again for the author the pursuit of what is reasonable is just as important as the claim of dogmatism. In fact they must be interwoven.

In the third place there is a candour that characterises every page, and every page is worth reading because the writer's ideas and comments on the broadest of religious issues are honest, and, for me, highly persuasive.

I would add one more reason for commending these pages. I have been convinced over long years, especially in preaching outdoors, that the proclamation of the Christian faith must, to a large extent, begin in a 'fellowship of controversy'. Controversy, at a time like this when we human beings are exposed to an ever-increasing bombardment of issues and problems, cannot be avoided. It must be welcomed.

Dr. Tattersall seems to me to be a model of that approach to belief which in the initial stage recognises, and indeed approves, the struggle with doubt. This is a valuable contribution to the ongoing quest for the Kingdom of Heaven as Jesus expounds it; and it is the more persuasive because it has the marks of struggle as well as the evidences of victory. I hope *A Doctor's Christianity* will be widely read. It should be.

Donald Soper

Introduction

I call this book *A Doctor's Christianity* because, as a retired physician, my understanding of God and mankind is necessarily influenced by my training and experience in life.

A doctor is concerned with several sorts of problems and many of these raise the question of 'purpose' in life; this is a religious issue. Many doctors are not church-going people, but few of us can avoid sometimes coming face to face with the religious problems of our patients.

Medical training requires a good doctor to develop a healthy degree of intelligent scepticism. "Truth lives at the bottom of a very deep well" is an axiom well appreciated in the medical world. I believe that it also applies to any serious attempt to understand Christianity!

This is not an erudite book. Christianity cannot be explained in its entirety; but undoubtedly there are some things about it that can. It is much more like 'falling in love' than passing an examination. Certainly, religious education at school is not usually enough to give a 'working knowledge' of it. To declare, "But the Bible says ..." is not good enough either, because that invites the question: "What does the Bible mean?" and this will often necessitate some careful searching to find out!

The Bishop of Salisbury drew the attention of his diocesan synod to "the confusion and lack of assurance about what it means to be a Christian".[1.]

This book is written with just such a person in mind, the ordinary intelligent person who may feel 'confused' or 'uncertain'. He probably thinks church rather dull. He may think church-going people show more concern for church buildings than for building up the Church; that they are more concerned to raise money than to use it wisely, and he may well prefer a measured philanthropy to a moment of prayer. So Mr Sensible Man supports charitable causes, he helps the chap who lives next door, he listens to his neighbour's laments rather than the liturgy, and eventually feels that he has done his bit for God.

Of course, we all know and like many such people! They could certainly liven up the Church; and if only church-going people could explain clearly why they go to church (which often they cannot!), then how interesting and instructive it all might be!

It is hoped that this book might help such people to sort things out a bit; especially those many people who aren't quite sure what Christianity is all about. I apologise unashamedly for my own theological shortcomings - I am a physician not a clergyman - and theologians must excuse this. I know, too, that some good church-people whom I greatly respect are bound to disagree with some of the ideas that I believe in and express. I ask for their tolerance; we are not clones, made to be all alike, and I am equally sure that other 'confused' people, such as Abou Ben Adam in Leigh Hunt's poem, will feel as uncertain as I do about some of these things. I have in mind especially those who do not have the time or opportunity for theological searching in their busy lives, because I do not believe that it is any more difficult to be an intelligent Christian than it is to be an intelligent lover!

Life is rather like a long journey with certain sign-posts: if we fail to see them it will help to read the map; and either way, the journey will be more satisfying and worthwhile if we can find out where we are going - that is, what we are living FOR. I believe that Christianity does have sign-posts, but some of them need repainting, and some of its maps need updating. I believe, too, that more than anything else, Christianity can help us not to get lost on the journey through life.

In this book, detailed references to, and quotations from the Bible are kept minimal. I deliberately omit reference to some subjects that seem to me of lesser importance, although I am well aware that they mean much more to other people. There are inevitably other omissions as well; I do not pretend to be writing a comprehensive book about religion.

John Hick in *Christianity at the Centre* has declared that the rise of modern science has made incredible much of the content of traditional Christian belief. I do believe that this statement is true for our modern world if Christianity is taken simply at face-value. But it is *not* just superstition or folklore. Jesus was concerned to teach mankind to grow away from primitive superstition. His teaching usually opposes the widespread magical animism that prevailed so widely in His time. Many people did not like it then; neither have they always liked it since. Folklore and superstition are very deeply rooted in human thought. The question Hick asks is important: "whether such beliefs are of the permanent essence of Christianity, or whether they belong to its development through a pre-scientific culture that has now passed into mankind's long history?"

How broadly or how narrowly does the Church interpret, for instance, the "Resurrection" or the "Incarnation"? They are certainly not of equal significance. These are matters that undoubtedly perplex thoughtful people today.

Religion is about belief, behaviour and God. This immediately raises questions that are closely related, in both the corporate and individual experience of mankind. At the present time "The Church" seems hesitant to offer guidance about this relationship. Perhaps this is because the structure of world society is changing so fast; but should the Church be bolder? The Church must always be seeking to elucidate truth, and to express it in contemporary language.

Although we live in a world of thought and ideas very different from that of two thousand years ago, or indeed only two hundred years ago, the profound teaching of Jesus Christ is just as significant for our generation as it was for those before our time.

Can we dispense with the overlay of folklore and superstition - not just to preserve Christianity, but to *clarify* it?

Reference.

1. Clifford Longley, (article) *The Times* 1.4.1989

How Christianity Began

The first section of this book deals with the amazing impact that Jesus Christ has had on the world.

After a great deal of wondering, the Resurrection is still a great mystery for which I can find no adequate acceptable explanation; but it is certainly at the centre of the whole issue of Christianity.

Knowing, as we now do, that the Gospels are unreliable as historical narrative, but that they seek to express religious truth, I believe that every man and woman needs to "find" Jesus Christ for themselves from these sources.

I believe that the Crucifixion is widely misunderstood. Surely it expresses the ordinary reaction of ordinary people when faced with something that is incomprehensible, and frightening or threatening. Undoubtedly Jesus' Ministry threatened many ordinary people who could not accept its consequences.

I believe that a good deal of misery is caused by the enthusiastic emphasis placed on "sudden" conversion. More often, there is a gradual growth in religious conviction, which resembles a seed germinating rather than a conjuring trick.

For many years I could not understand St Paul. However, modern translations of the Epistles, and various excellent commentaries, have helped me a lot. Happily, there are now many books which do explain his teaching far better than I can.

The Resurrection of Jesus Christ

Christianity did not begin in a stable in Bethlehem; it began with a very strange mystery that occurred after the Crucifixion, and which led to the development of the Early Church. There is no satisfactory explanation of this mystery. Within the present limits of human understanding it is still an unresolved problem. The more closely one examines it, the more difficult it becomes. But it is the mystery of the Resurrection which has given rise to the development of the Christian Church which, through the Christian Religion, has exerted an immense influence on human thought and world-wide human affairs. That is why the Resurrection merits very careful appraisal.

There is no more emotive subject among Christian people, perhaps because it touches so closely upon the hopes of personal eternity, or perhaps because piety seems to forbid thoughtful consideration of such a fundamental doctrine.

Resurrection Concepts Prevalent at the Time of Jesus Christ.

It is necessary to be aware of some of the religious ideas that prevailed among the Mediterranean people about the time of Jesus Christ. Magical Animism was widespread. The belief that human life was perpetual unless interrupted by either an act of God, accident or sorcery, had been widely accepted for centuries in many pagan communities (see Genesis Ch. 2.3; Ch. 3.4; Ch. 3.22). The rites associated with the worship of Attis, Dionysius and Osiris all incorporate a primitive belief in resurrection. Such beliefs are very deeply rooted in primitive religion all over the world, as has been shown by Freud [1.] and Fraser.[2, 3.] The various Gods in Greek mythology were frequently in the habit of visiting the earth, behaving as human beings for a while, then returning to Mount Olympus (c.f. Acts of the Apostles, Ch. 14, 11-15).

Judaism at the time of Christ was certainly monotheistic, but its beliefs about resurrection are uncertain: Sadducees on the whole disbelieved in a life after death, but many Jews (especially the Pharisees) held that the Second Coming of the Messiah would usher in the "End of Time", when graves would yield up their dead for judgement together with the living. Following this, "The Just" (ie those having a right relationship with God) would proceed to eternal life because "time" as we understand it would then have come to an end (cf Daniel, Ch. 12, 2-4). The Judaic eschatological association of the "Coming of the Messiah" with the "End of Time" is an important indication of the uncertainty about life after death in Jewish thought.

It is necessary, too, to be clear that certain Biblical stories (myth) are not instances of resurrection in the Christian sense of the Resurrection of Jesus Christ, because the human subjects in these stories are restored to *ordinary physical life,* allowing for normal physical death to follow later (eg Lazarus; the widow of Nain's son; Jairus' daughter).

Inevitably, these and other pre-Christian ideas on resurrection influenced Christianity and led to a misunderstanding of the quite different Christian use of the term

Resurrection. None of these older, more primitive uses of the term resurrection carry the Christian belief in the utterly unexpected Resurrection of an executed and abandoned Person (Jesus Christ) to a life of on-going activity that would altogether transcend any sort of subsequent physical death. Nevertheless, many people are confused by the difference between these different concepts of Resurrection, and this difference is not sufficiently emphasised in Christian teaching.

The Starting Point.

For any proper consideration of the Resurrection of Jesus Christ, it is essential to begin with facts that are beyond dispute.[3] It can be generally agreed that someone called Jesus of Nazareth lived in Palestine about two thousand years ago and was executed in Jerusalem. Thus his "cause" should have been crushed and his followers dispersed. Why did that not happen?

It is an undoubted fact that within very few years of the Crucifixion, people in different places around the Eastern Mediterranean were meeting to celebrate that this Jesus was alive, having "risen" from the dead. That is how the Christian religion began and it probably started quite soon after the crucifixion. These little groups increased in number, and for convenience we call them the Early Church. They spread very rapidly; within thirty years of Jesus' execution they were established in many places throughout the Roman Empire.

What had really happened between the Crucifixion and the earliest beginnings of the Early Church for this quite extraordinary belief to have spread so widely and so rapidly? It is necessary to examine the New Testament reports that refer to this strange phenomenon, because there is no other source.

New Testament Extracts.

The following very short passages are derived from each of the gospels to indicate that although they are all describing something uniquely extraordinary, nevertheless they differ considerably in detail:

In St Mark: (Ch. 15, 40 - Ch. 16, 9), Joseph buries the body in a rock tomb with two or three women watching. The day after the Sabbath the women return to anoint the body but find the stone rolled away allowing entry. A young man within frightens them, and tells them that Jesus has been raised, before pointing to the place where his body had been. He tells them to go and tell the disciples and Peter that they will see Jesus in Galilee as he had told them (14, 28). The women flee but tell nobody.

In St Matthew: (Ch. 27, 55 - Ch. 28, 20), the women are named differently, and the story has an internal contradiction about the guards sleeping outside the tomb but nevertheless allowing the body to be stolen! (Such a rumour was current in Jewish circles in reaction to Christian resurrection claims). The women only came to visit the tomb; they see the stone moved during an earthquake by an angel who stayed outside. The account closes with the disciples going to Galilee to receive their missionary charge there.

In St Luke: (Ch. 23, 55 - Ch. 24, 53), women from Galilee, who are named later, prepare to anoint but find the tomb open and empty; they are approached by two men in white who remind them that, from Galilee, Jesus had prophesied that he would rise (Mark 9, 31). The women recollect, and go to tell the disciples who do not believe them. "He led them out as far as to Bethany ... (Ch. 24, 50), and while he blessed them he was carried up into Heaven."

In St John: (Ch. 19, 38 - Ch. 20, 29), the women do not go to the burial. Joseph is joined by Nicodemus and the body is anointed before being placed in the tomb. On the day after the Sabbath, Mary Magdalene comes to the tomb alone, presumably to visit. On observing the stone rolled away she immediately runs to Peter and "the other disciple" who both run to the tomb. Peter is the first of them to enter. They believe, then they go. Mary has waited, then she peeps in and sees two angels. On turning round she sees Jesus, and when He speaks her name she is convinced.

It is essential to add to these four different gospel accounts some extracts written by St Paul, because these Pauline references pre-date the gospel accounts by at least twenty years and therefore demonstrate that the Christian Resurrection traditions were certainly widely held at least two decades before the earliest gospel was written.

In St Paul: (I Cor Ch. 15): St Paul refers to when he was in Corinth earlier (possibly as early as 50AD) and he had handed on to the people there the account of the Resurrection which he had been given... He describes what is regarded as the oldest tradition, viz: that Christ was raised on the third day. However, Paul continues: (I Cor Ch. 15, 5), "that He was seen by Peter, then by "the twelve" (this term is often used referring to the Apostles even after the death of Judas), then by over 500 people at once (a very large number indeed for the Early Church in any one place) (Cf Acts 1, 15), then by James, and afterwards by all the Apostles and finally by Paul himself.

It is not necessary to quote the dozen or so other Resurrection references in St Paul's epistles; they add little, but they do reiterate the meaning of what Paul wrote in I Cor. Ch. 15.

Comment on these New Testament Extracts.

The foregoing extracts, abbreviated though they are, all agree in that they refer to something very remarkable relating to the on-going activity of Jesus Christ after the Crucifixion. All these accounts were originally written, and probably embellished later, by people and for people whose normal way of thinking was quite different from Mr Modern Man. Those people accepted the "truth" of symbol and myth far more readily than would happen today. They were less critical, and did not expect factual proof. Those writers were not like journalists trained to write for a modern newspaper!

Allowance must be made, too, for the very difficult linguistic problem (in any language) of describing a vivid religious experience using any form of words. It is the same sort of linguistic difficulty as trying to describe music, emotion or wonder within the constraint of mere words, and this is further compounded by the ordinary difficulties of translation into English from the original Greek.

We have to make the best of the information available; there were no eye-witnesses who actually *saw* the Resurrection first-hand with their eyes. The evidence is all circumstantial. It is remarkable even today to realise that such widely varying opinions are held by persons of high intelligence and integrity regarding the available accounts of the Resurrection. As J A Baker comments prosaically: "Readers tend to find the accounts convincing or otherwise according to their presuppositions. This is nothing new." [4.]

The fundamental difficulty is whether the New Testament narratives concern an objective event that factually happened (ie a 'body' leaving a tomb), or whether they are referring to vivid subjective experiences perceived (or 'seen') by a large number of people.

The Empty Tomb.

Many people are convinced of the objective reality of the Resurrection stories for the very reason that these do *not* all exactly agree! If four people witness a road accident from four different points it is not to be expected that they will give identical descriptions of exactly what happened. (Many failures to prosecute a motorist after an accident occur because there is insufficient corroboration to convince a jury.) Thus, many people are impressed, because of the discrepancies, that the gospel writers are telling a factual story; that the Resurrection of a dead body did occur. Supporters of this view are influenced by the empty tomb as "evidence"; but the body could have been stolen or secretly re-buried! Such a finding does not signify a Resurrection such as the disciples proclaimed.

It has been said that if the body of Jesus had been displayed undergoing decomposition, such a demonstration could have discredited the whole Resurrection belief. Maybe; but it is nevertheless very difficult to conjecture how such a very improbable story could have been invented without an empty tomb being left behind. Why was the body not produced? Because it had "risen"!

So if the physical body "rose", then what happened to it later? St Matthew and St Luke attempt to resolve this problem by postulating the Ascension: Luke says from Bethany, Matthew says from seventy miles to the north, in Galilee.

Perhaps the most difficult problem that has to be explained by those who accept the bodily resurrection as a factual event must be to find any credible reason why the resurrected body of Jesus was not seen by any unbelievers, or indeed by the world at large.

There is certainly evidence that the belief in an empty tomb is a very early tradition of the Early Church. If so, then it is very odd that St Paul, who was absolutely convinced that there was a Resurrection, never mentions it! Could the story have been perceived by him as irrelevant to the essential truth? Hans Kung,[6] the eminent modern theologian, has declared that the Tomb Stories are merely legends, added later to provoke amazement. If so, then the Resurrection is undoubtedly misunderstood by many Christians today.

The Appearances.

Just what is meant by the "appearances" of Jesus after the Resurrection? (Matthew: Ch. 28; Mk: Ch. 16; Luke: Ch. 24; John, Ch. 20 & 21). There are linguistic problems and uncertainty regarding the finer nuances. Are we dealing with some kind of visual hallucinations? Not one of these "appearances" carries any sort of description of what Jesus looked like, which is surprising. He was simply "recognised". The accounts seem to imply some sort of experience which is not simply hallucinatory but which is also different from an intellectual acceptance that the "cause" of Jesus was sound and is continuing. The "appearance" of Jesus seems to provoke action: the women in Mark's gospel are told to go; a missionary charge is spelt out in Matthew's gospel; the women do go in Luke's; and the Emmaus walkers also go to tell their experience. In John's gospel, Thomas does believe, and the disciples do catch fish when instructed how to cast their nets. St Paul is a transformed person, and so is Mary Magdalene. In each case an experience enables each person to *see*, that is, to 'see' in the sense of perceiving a "revelation". Is this not perhaps similar to a scholar at school suddenly understanding something new - a completely new, difficult idea; or the famous cry of Archimedes: "Eureka!"?

So was the Resurrection a factual event in the life of Jesus, *or* was it a decisive historical moment in the spiritual life of each disciple? Certainly the Jesus of the Resurrection appearances was no mere ghostly apparition to those disciples who saw, recognised, and even touched Him. They all confidently identified the resurrected Jesus with Jesus of Nazareth whom they had known in His lifetime.

What, Then, Really is the Easter Message?

Our only factual information about Jesus derives from the New Testament, and the Resurrection "evidence" comprises only biased, circumstantial accounts, yet their impact on mankind has been enormous.

Not one of the Resurrection traditions discloses any specific or new information about God as the Creator, or "First Cause" of the Universe. Mankind knows no more, no less, about the nature of God because of the Resurrection than our forefathers knew before it.

Nevertheless, the Resurrection phenomenon so dramatically changed the thought and action of the disciples that they forthwith proclaimed both that Jesus Christ had "risen", and also the message of the Christian gospel as they had come progressively to understand it. They could only express it in the thought-language of their time; they had no other option.

Suppose that Jesus had been like Judas Maccabaeus 150 years earlier, an enthusiastic man of patriotic ambition. Is it conceivable that those disciples would have constructed such a strange belief about such a man? It is an unavoidable feature of the Resurrection tradition that the unique quality of Jesus' human life and ministry played a central part in constituting this very strange belief - even though our known accounts of it were only written down many years later. Baker[5] has emphasised that the proper significance of the Resurrection cannot be detached from Jesus' Ministry and the ensuing Crucifixion. It is a belief that arises from the impact of all three events - it is certainly not a fairy-tale tagged on!

No reasoned argument can refute that the Resurrection phenomenon utterly transformed the lives of those earliest disciples and the Early Church, and it seems to have been transforming the lives of Christian people ever since. I believe that this is the real enigma and mystery of the Resurrection, from which the tremendous influence of the Christian religion on mankind has undoubtedly developed.

References.

1. Freud, S. *Totem and Taboo* (1919); in English: Pelican (1938).
2. Fraser, J.G. *Folk Lore in the Old Testament* Macmillan & Co (1923).
3. Fraser, J.G. *The Golden Bough* Macmillan & Co. (1922).
4. Baker, J.A. *The Foolishness of God* Darton, Longman & Todd (1970) p. 251.
5. Baker, J.A. op, cit. p.266
6. Kung, Hans *Christ Sein* R. Piper Verlag (1974), English trans. Fount paperback (1978)

The Ministry of Jesus Christ

The Ministry of Jesus Christ will be considered from three aspects. Firstly, the quality of the evidence that is available about Jesus must be evaluated. How reliable is it? How much of the information is circumstantial or second-hand? How much is myth, and if so why does it remain there as myth?

Secondly, what exactly did Jesus teach? What does His message (gospel) actually have to say? How much of its content was "new", and to what extent was He merely repeating, but perhaps more clearly, what the more devout of the Jewish people had believed for many generations?

Thirdly, what sort of man was Jesus during the three or four year period (or possibly less) of His teaching and preaching in Palestine? It is reasonable to consider these matters in the order stated.

The Extraneous Evidence About Jesus.

Apart from the New Testament, references to the actual existence of Jesus are remarkably scarce. The Jewish historian, Josephus (AD 37 - ?95) is generally agreed to be reasonably accurate by the standards of those days. In his *Jewish Antiquities*, a work of twenty volumes covering the history of the Jews from their earliest times up to the outbreak of the war with Rome (c. 66 AD), he makes no determinative mention of Jesus, but refers to "the stoning of James, the brother of Jesus, the so-called

Christ".[1] Suetonius (75 - 150 AD), refers to trouble with the Christians in Rome during the reign of Claudius (41 - 54 AD) "because they were constantly rioting at the instigation of Chrestus" (but it is not clear whether he thought Chrestus was someone alive in Rome at the time, as both Hans King and Paul Johnson remark.[1, 2]) Pliny the younger, writing in 112 AD states: "the sect sang a hymn to Christ as a God."[1, 2]

Thus there is scant evidence from non-Christian sources that Jesus was a real person who actually lived. Scanty indeed, but the evidence is about as good as the independent evidence that Socrates or Confucius or Buddha ever lived, and certainly better than the evidence for the existence of King Arthur, or any other notable British individual alive at the time of Christ.

The only definite evidence for the actual existence of Jesus derives from the gospels in the New Testament, and to a lesser extent in the Epistles.

These internal sources must be examined because that is where the substance of Jesus' teaching is to be found, and the only source from which we can find clues as to the sort of man He really was.

The Three Synoptic Gospels.

The accounts attributed to St Matthew, St Mark and St Luke were written at least forty years after Jesus died. So just how reliable can such evidence be?

Obviously, if during all those forty years after His death there had been no mention of Jesus among his followers, then there would be no Christianity today.

There is abundant evidence from history that those forty years covered a period of enthusiastic and vigorous missionary activity, with the rapid spread of Christianity around the Mediterranean region. With such widespread religious activities it is inconceivable that *nothing* was written about it! But authority disagreement with such expressed opinions could undoubtedly have provoked their suppression. Probably, too, the hope of a second coming of Christ, which was widespread among those early Christians, was an even stronger deterrent; but as this hope waned, particularly after the destruction of Jerusalem by Titus in AD 70, and also the expulsion of Christians from Jewish synagogues around 80 AD, there was an increased incentive to write down recollections about Jesus.

Modern investigation of the three synoptic texts has established that Mark is the oldest, and that Matthew and Luke derive substantially from it. Mark contains 661 verses, and 606 of these are reproduced in Matthew's 1,068 verses. In Luke's gospel there are 1,149 verses, of which 320 derive from Mark, leaving only about 24 verses in Mark which are not reproduced in either Matthew or Luke.[3.] Today it is accepted that the authors of both Matthew and Luke made use of Mark's text quite freely. It remains uncertain whether the version that we know as Mark's gospel is the original; there could be a common precursor of all three synoptic gospels written by an unknown author at about the time of the destruction of Jerusalem in 70 AD.

It is a common mistake to think that the synoptic gospels in some way constitute a biography of Jesus. They are religious, not historical, writings, and they comprise stories, quotations and teachings, remembered perhaps over a period of forty years. They are reminiscent in some ways of old soldiers recollecting a wartime commander, emphasising his qualities either from their own memories or from impressions they received from someone else; and not necessarily reliable as factual history. Real historians hardly existed two thousand years ago!

It is easy to read these gospels and perceive how the text sometimes switches abruptly to a different recollection, often quite different in terms of time, place and style. Frequently their object is to transmit amazement as well as religious instruction. It must also be remembered that these old documents have been copied out several times at least, and so include some well-meaning editing.

The Gospel according to St John.

St John's Gospel is altogether different in style. It was probably written around 100 AD. (Some experts nevertheless believe it may precede the synoptic gospels.) It was written for non-Jewish (rather than Jewish) readers, whereas the synoptists were more orientated towards Jewish readers. They describe an itinerant Ministry that could have lasted about three years, but John recounts events that could have all occurred within approximately three weeks. Whereas the synoptists relate Jesus' stories and teaching, John gives the more vivid portrayal of Jesus as a real living Person.

What Exactly Did Jesus Teach?

It is not my purpose to discuss details of the gospels. Much excellent literature is available and anyone can, and certainly should, read one of the synoptic gospels right through in an English translation. They are most easily understood in a modern, more colloquial version. The glorious beauty of the cadences in the Authorised Version is, like Shakespeare's language, beyond dispute. Today unfortunately, the subtleties and nuances of early seventeenth century English can be easily missed, and the real meaning of the original Greek is often clearer in a good modern paraphrase. Nowadays, the Greek texts are essential only for scholars and theologians.

St Mark's gospel is a relatively terse record that can be read inside an hour; St Matthew's links its content even more closely to the Old Testament than does Mark; I think (as do many people) that St Luke's gospel is the warmest and most readable of the three. Matthew (Ch. 5, 6, 7) contains the famous Sermon on the Mount, and Luke has the two most famous stories told by Jesus: the parables of the Good Samaritan(Ch. 10), and the Prodigal Son (Ch. 15).

The Old Testament is important because it recounts the religious history of the Jewish People, the moral and social rules which they were enjoined to respect and obey, and their aspirations for their future as a nation. Although never a world power, they dreamed of being such and hoped that their Messiah would bring this about. That was their problem with Jesus. He was a Jew, and his alleged genealogy was beyond reproach - which was important to Jews. He was undoubtedly a good man; and He was a religious man. The dilemma was whether He was the long hoped-for Messiah. Their difficulty with him was that He did not keep strictly to their religious rules, but nevertheless taught authoritatively about their Judaic religion. So what were they to do?

Jesus consistently taught that a person-to-person relationship of respect and compassion is what matters in life's affairs, and that to live by such principles releases everyone from the tedium of meticulous deference to the ancient Jewish law. This is the devastating topsy-turvy revolution in human relationships which He boldly affirmed as the real truth of God's Law, and the best way for humankind to live with one another.

What Sort of Man Was Jesus?

Undoubtedly, the simplest and best answer is to read the marvellous word-picture spelt out for us by the Gospel attributed to St John. It portrays a character who commands both respect and reverence as no other Person does in all literature, either secular or religious. It needs to be read leisurely, and such a reading imparts a feeling that this man is unique, a Leader of supreme moral strength and religious power who can therefore be called "Son of God".

To illustrate this, two modern passages will be quoted: one, by Lord Beaverbrook, the newspaper magnate, and the other a well-known exposition by the famous author, H.G. Wells. Wells devotes no less than eight pages of his famous *Outline of History* to describing the

Ministry of Jesus, which passage concludes: "He was too great for His disciples ... Perhaps the priests and rulers and the rich men understood Him better than His followers. He was like a terrible moral huntsman digging mankind out of the snug burrows in which they had lived hitherto. Is it any wonder that the priests realised that between this man and themselves there was no choice but that He or the priestcraft should perish? For to take Him seriously was to enter upon a strange and alarming life, to abandon habits, to control instincts and impulses, to essay an incredible happiness..."[4.]

Beaverbrook writes: "The Mission of Christ as revealed in the Gospels was to tell mankind how to achieve happiness in this world...The Kingdom is a state of mind into which a man enters in this life ... It does not concern itself with systems of government; it does not matter whether the man who possesses it is rich or poor ... Christ spoke directly to the individual soul offering that peace and happiness which the material world cannot bring ... selfishness, narrowness, hypocrisy, self-seeking are shown to be the sure precursors of misery, and their antithesis the road to joy. Jesus was neither a theologian nor a communist. He was the Son of God who came to give comfort to our souls; to teach us how we could live in this world with the most supreme happiness..."[5.] Beaverbrook may not have got it quite right but it is certainly good enough for many people!

So the priests brought Him to Pontius Pilate who ordered his execution. Why exactly they did this may be debatable, but it certainly distracts attention from the teaching of Jesus.

References.

1. Hans Kung *On Being a Christian* (Collins) 1978 p. 119-120
2. Paul Johnson *A History of Christianity* (Penguin) 1976 p.22
3. William Barclay *The Gospel of St Mark* (St Andrews Press) p.24
4. H.G. Wells *The Outline of History* (Cassell & Co.) 1920, p.531
5. Lord Beaverbrook *The Divine Propagandist*.

The Execution of Jesus Christ

Why was Jesus crucified? The answer is not as obvious as many sermons suggest.

Anyone trying to understand Jesus should have read at least one of the synoptic gospels, as well as St John's gospel. It is important to remember not only that these accounts are biased, but that they were certainly edited, and probably considerably edited, during the century or so after they were written. The abbreviated paraphrases about the Resurrection which have been quoted earlier exemplify the sort of discrepancies that abound in the gospels.

Similar discrepancies can also be found in the descriptions of the events in the last week of Jesus' life as these are recounted in the gospels. It must be emphasised that the gospels are not narrative; they were written and edited to teach about Jesus, to invoke wonder and amazement, and to encourage the worship of the Early Church. So with regard to accurate detail and sequence, the events of the last week of Jesus' life must be accepted with suitable caution.

Of Jesus' summary execution, in an utter travesty of justice after a hurried and rigged trial, there can be no doubt. (If indeed the arrest, interrogation by the Jewish High Priests during the night, and the sentence passed the next day by the Roman Governor, who declared the case against Jesus to be unproved, can be called a trial in any ordinary legal sense.)

Before suggesting the real reason why Jesus *was* executed, some of the reasons often put forward must be considered, because they are probably not correct.

Judas Iscariot.

For many centuries, the treachery of Judas in betraying Jesus was widely believed to be responsible for the crucifixion. To hold such a view requires us to believe the incompetence of the Roman soldiery to keep order among an excited crowd, or the reluctance of a Roman governor to enforce order, and it ignores the antagonism of the Jewish priesthood towards Jesus. It overlooks the obvious fact that Jesus moved freely among the crowds in Jerusalem who were gathering for the Passover and so he could have been arrested at any time. There is no hint in the biblical accounts that Jesus would have "passed through the midst of them" (Lk. Ch. 4, 30) as he did earlier at Nazareth when threatened by a hostile mob. Nor is there reason to suppose that Judas was a deliberately wicked man or predestined to fulfil an evil role in the closing events of Jesus' life. The gospel accounts were written soon after the expulsion of Christians from the Jewish synagogues, and because of this are undoubtedly biased against the Jews, probably blaming them unduly for their alleged part in the pre-crucifixion events. Judas probably longed for the *Messiah* to come, and for him to lead a successful rebellion against the power of Rome, similar to the uprising a century or so earlier led by Judas Maccabaeus, which had failed. As Jesus' Ministry unfolded, Judas probably feared that Jesus would betray those nationalist Jewish aspirations - climbing down at the last moment - and he would have been utterly dismayed at the prospect of his beloved Leader "letting the side down" in such a way. Undoubtedly a great many of Jesus' followers shared Judas' hopes, probably those who misunderstood the true meaning of "The Kingdom of Heaven is at hand".

Pontius Pilate.

We can justifiably wonder how incompetent Pilate really was. His ineptitude is suggested in many verses in the gospels: Matthew Ch. 27, particularly v. 18-19, and v. 22-24; Mark Ch. 15, 14; Luke Ch. 23, particularly 13 - 16, and 22 -24; and John Ch. 18, 31 and 38, also Ch. 19, 6, 10, 12, etc. It makes much more sense to surmise that these passages were inserted later to exonerate a Roman administration from possible Christian castigation, directed then at the Jews, whom they held responsible for the Crucifixion. (Around 80 AD the Christians had enough problems without suggesting a Roman judicial murder as well!)

Ransom.

The idea that Jesus died in some way to "ransom", to purchase or redeem human beings expresses a primitive animistic belief (Ex. Ch. 21, 30; Ps, 49, 7, etc.). It was still widely believed at the time of Christ, although its origins are to be found in ancient Magical Animism.

The Atonement.

This theological doctrine is also related to the notion of ransom, denoting the necessity (theologically) for a means of some form of reparation for sin, leading to reconciliation between man and God. It, too, finds its origins in ancient animistic religion and, in my view this, as it is often stated, has little Christian significance today.

Sacrifice.

For two thousand years theologians have been putting forward a variety of explanations as to who Jesus really was, and why He went to Calvary. Such ideas are most frequently expressed in terms of either Old Testament Judaism or in Greek ways of thought. This generation thinks differently from our ancestors; concepts such as "paying the price of sin", which certainly troubled the latter, seem outdated to us. Today we do not think in terms of seeking God's approval by human sacrifice, or obtaining forgiveness by sacrificing animals on an altar instead of human beings. It seems rather crude and primitive. But to Jews, and many others two thousand years ago, that habit of sacrifice had been completely acceptable for many generations. That does not mean that we should go on for evermore trying to understand and use outworn concepts. We need new clothes when the old ones wear out!

So, Why Was Jesus Crucified?

Nobody can know with certainty; the question led to great perplexity among the early leaders of the Church, and much foolish behaviour down the ages by various sorts of misguided people. Concern about who Jesus was has distracted many generations from the relevance of what He had to teach mankind. Twenty centuries later, two suggestions can be made in terms of our own contemporary way of thought, which seem to me to make better sense in our time:

Firstly, when we contemplate thoughtfully the life of Jesus Christ, and acknowledge in humility how very little we really know about Him, we are surely filled with wonder and reverence for the sort of Person he was, and the profound things He taught. Even if much of our information is distorted (and this should be more widely recognised than it is), if we nevertheless find Jesus not only credible but marvellous in His life and teaching as we can understand them from the gospels, then He is certainly showing us somethings that He confidently believed about God - so much that it is *something He was prepared to die for.*

Every schoolchild knows how difficult it can be to swim against the tide of peer opinion. In the religious world we have recently seen Dr David Jenkins, the outgoing Bishop of Durham being cheaply ridiculed, often by those who do not take the trouble to try to understand him. A century ago, Charles Gore and the other contributors to *Lux Mundi* were similarly criticised. In the middle of the nineteenth century, Frederick Temple, then

Headmaster of Rugby School and later Archbishop of Canterbury, edited *Essays and Reviews* as a result of which there was violent protest when he was consecrated a bishop. One contributor to *Essays and Reviews,* John Colenso, the Bishop of Natal, was excommunicated for his radical views. (see also page 166)

Similar popular reaction occurs in all realms of human activity, whenever entrenched customs or beliefs are thought to be attacked or criticised, and this has been the case many, many times in human affairs, from Socrates to Charles Darwin. Jesus' teaching was provocative, and the response was to be expected.

Secondly, Christianity is described as a *revealed* religion because it was made known by Jesus Christ to our forefathers, and through them to us. Jesus brought to mankind a new way of looking at the events of life, a better way of living, and He declared these things with a self-confidence that inevitably aroused hate and animosity from those whose *modus vivendi* was threatened. His teaching continues to disturb ordinary human affairs today.

I believe that one can discern in the unfolding of God's marvellous Creation, millennium by millennium, a very gradual change occurring in mankind's understanding - not of God, but certainly of mankind's relationship, one human being with another...

Geology, archeology and anthropology have much to teach us about this wonderful world that God has created, but these disciplines and their insights still seem to make but little impact on theology. There was a time when *Homo Sapiens* first recognised the possibility of God, became *Homo Religiosus*, and began to wonder what God was like. Jesus Christ offers us the best interpretation available within our present limits of human understanding, and so our forefathers called Him the "Son of God".

Were they all wrong? Or were they showing profound insight? To use a metaphor from current scientific jargon - does the Revelation given to us through the Life, Ministry and Resurrection of Jesus Christ correspond in some way to a mutation in the ever-upward evolution of *Homo Religiosus?*

References.

The Golden Bough (abb. edition) J.G. Fraser (1922)
Folklore in the Old Testament J.G. Fraser (1923)
The Christian Agnostic L.D. Weatherhead (1965)
The Rise of Christianity E.W. Barnes (1945)
The Phenomenon of Man P. Teilhard de Chardin (Collins) 1959

The Nature of Religious Conversion

The mystery of the Resurrection of Jesus Christ has been considered as the beginning of Christianity, but only because it was somehow validated by His unique Ministry which culminated in a totally unjustified execution by Crucifixion.

But Christianity did not end there. It goes on and on down the centuries; it has dominated the principles of nations and peoples, and affected the lives of countless individual men and women; this extraordinary influence has impinged on the whole pattern of Western Civilisation for two thousand years. It is called Religious Conversion.

Psychological Background.

Religious Conversion has been defined as "a change from lack of faith to religious belief" or "from one religion to another" (Collins Dictionary). But faith and belief are by no means simple concepts. The human mind, or psyche, is very complex, and never more so than when seeking to understand the faith or belief of someone else's psyche.

It was a strange experience sixty years ago for an English boy to observe the behaviour of a gathering of many thousands at a Nazi rally addressed by Hitler. It is bewildering for parents when an adolescent son or daughter "falls into the clutches of" (a biased phrase) the Moonies, the Scientology Church, or a similar cult. Brain-washing is now well-recognised as a real psychic phenomenon, and William Sargant[1] has declared that today the technique is sufficiently understood for it to be possible deliberately to alter a man's thought patterns, or moral code, and instil in him utterly different loyalties and beliefs. Sargant has warned of the danger to society generally if such techniques should ever be adopted on a large scale for unscrupulous political ends.

Hypnosis was used in Persia and India (and probably far more widely by primitive 'medicine men' for thousands of years), before Mesmer raised medical interest in the subject in Europe during the eighteenth century. Hypnosis certainly can have medical uses, and I have used it successfully many times in the treatment of asthma. It has been used for a variety of medical purposes, and very many times to achieve anaesthesia, particularly for dental extractions. There are excellent medical treatises dealing with the subject more fully.

Religious Conversion, too, may be a psychological phenomenon not far removed from very complex and possibly dangerous psychic mechanisms. Many people have witnessed "marvellous conversions" at deeply emotional evangelistic meetings; to what extent are these but fickle responses of the mind, or conversely, a deeply sincere and genuine response of the human spirit? The sub-conscious mechanisms of the human mind must be remembered and kept in perspective when seeking to understand religious conversion.

"Ye Must Be Born Again"

So what does "Ye must be born again" mean nowadays? There are at least two yard-sticks that can usefully be remembered, and both are vividly illustrated in the New Testament. In John's gospel, Ch. 3, we read that Nicodemus, a ruler of the Jews, came to Jesus by night enquiring (curiosity?) about The Kingdom of God, only to be told "Ye must be born again" (Ch. 3,7) (explanation?).

In Acts Ch. 5, St Peter was (as we might say today), an effusive and enthusiastic evangelist, provoking the responsible authorities to such limits that his very life was endangered. Then Gamliel, a doctor of law, advised the Sanhedrin to be moderate: "If this work be of men it will come to naught, but if it be of God ye cannot overthrow it."

Nicodemus, with his important question, and Gamaliel with his cautious guidance, each display shrewd wisdom with regard to religious conversion. A modern English psychiatrist, Jack Dominian, has pointed out that after the physical body has reached adult life, *it still needs to discover its spiritual self.*

Carl Gustav Jung[2] puts it this way: "Human thought cannot conceive any system of final truth that could give a man what he needs in order to live: ie faith, hope, love and insight...These four highest achievements are so many gifts of grace, and they come through experience (acceptance?) which is something given. The way to this experience is rather an adventure which requires us to commit ourselves with our whole being."

I believe that four stages are discernible in the way the human mind arrives at religious conversion. The individual concerned has to be inquisitive, and to reflect on the matter to the extent that led Nicodemus to enquire of Jesus by night, and the enquiry must be satisfactorily answered in some way, just as Jesus answered Nicodemus. The third feature about the unfolding of Religious Conversion I call "acceptance", by which I mean that the psyche of the individual must accept the explanation that has been offered in response to his curiosity. This is not by any means always the case, and such acceptance does not necessarily imply an intellectual acceptance (eg Thomas in John, Ch. 20, 28). It may be an expression of highly-charged emotion. The final stage of conversion implies some sort of commitment which may be expressed in many ways; its manifestation has varied through the centuries. Essentially, Christian "commitment" nowadays means doing something or giving something that is felt in some way to be serving, on behalf of, Jesus Christ.

Surely Dominian and Jung are both echoing our Lord's words: "Ye must be born again", but in modern parlance? The physically mature human being certainly does need to find (his or her) spiritual maturity to become a balanced and complete person; and not everybody does attain such maturity, even in a whole lifetime. What a person needs in order to live fully is to be really committed to the adventure of life.

This is the challenge which the Gospel of Jesus Christ offers us. He put it: "Ye must be born again", or make a commitment to the discovery of spiritual life. We call it religious conversion. It is a mysterious experience, something like falling in love! Some men and women come together as a friendship matures; for others it is love at first sight. Similarly, in the matter of religious conversion our own individual experiences differ widely.

The Bible instances many examples of religious conversion, for example in the Old Testament: Moses and the burning bush (Ex. Ch. 3, 2 ff); The Call of Samuel (I Sam. Ch. 3, 4 ff); Isaiah's Vision (Is. Ch. 6, 8 ff); Jeremiah's Mission (Jer. Ch. 1, 6 ff) and so on. There are plenty more to be found in the New Testament.

Eight Miles to Emmaus.

Of the New Testament passages, I find the walk to Emmaus (Lk. Ch. 24, 13-32) is a marvellous allegory. This great story is commonly regarded as one of the post-resurrection appearances. It is more profound to examine it as a remarkable description of the nature of religious conversion. The story comprises four sections:

FIRST. Two disciples are walking back home from Jerusalem, a distance of about eight miles, say, two hours' walking. They are displaying signs of inquisitiveness: "They talked together of all these things which had happened", the extraordinary events in Jerusalem, viz. Jesus' trial and crucifixion. "They communed and reasoned". In other words, their religious *curiosity* and interest have certainly been aroused.

SECOND. Jesus joins them (but "their eyes were holden that they should not know Him"), and He asks what they were talking about that made them sad. Cleopas answers by stating the facts, including "but we trusted that it had been He which should have redeemed Israel". (They seem to admit their problem here - did they, like Judas Iscariot, also misunderstand Jesus' meaning of "The Kingdom of Heaven is at hand"?) Then Jesus *explains* their problems for them, beginning: "O fools to believe all that the prophets have spoken..." and continuing: "He expounded unto them in all the Scriptures the things concerning himself".

THIRD. They do not allow their casual companion to go on his way when they reach home; instead they invite him to supper - so we can infer that, following his explanation He is a welcome guest: "Abide with us for the day is far spent", and then they suddenly *accept* Him when He breaks the bread. In no way was the incident regarded as magic, supernatural or miraculous.

FOURTH. It led to immediate action: they have just come home and had supper; also "the day was far spent". Yet then "they rose up the same hour" and walked the eight miles back to Jerusalem, to tell the other disciples there of their experience. *Commitment?*

Of course many modern Christians can, and do, walk to Emmaus without going to Palestine! Religious Conversion (like falling in love) often begins with a period of enquiry and then explanation; acceptance may follow - but not necessarily immediately - and if so, commitment confirms it. For some people, but not all, this is highly charged with emotion, sometimes at the time, sometimes later.

If this allegorical understanding of the Emmaus story is plausible, is it too great a stretch of imagination to discern a similar, though less clear, exposition in the other gospel stories about the happenings between the Crucifixion and the formation of the Early Church? Women would not have gone to the tomb if they didn't care; the young man or angel proffers some kind of explanation; emotional involvement is described (terror, amazement); the appearance of Jesus convinces...I believe that the post-Crucifixion appearances of Jesus are the earliest examples of Christian Conversion. The real 'miracle' of Christianity, the mystery of the Resurrection, is that similar conversion experiences have been going on ever since. As E W Barnes[3] puts it, "Out of apparently dead formulae and empty ritual the Spirit of Christ emerges, as buds in springtime appear on what seemed lifeless twigs...So His followers are led to claim for Jesus Christ a supremacy that time cannot end. Because his Spirit does not die, they worship Him as Son of God."

There seems to be no comparable phenomenon in non-Christian religious history. A case can be made out that the four stages of the Emmaus Story indicate the strange way 'conversion' unfolds. Curiosity, or uncertainty about one's aims in life, is an essential feature at the beginning. People who are completely content with their situation in life seem to me very unlikely to experience religious conversion. Similarly, those who know *nothing* of Christianity have no opportunity to convert. It is concern about such persons that has given ardour and vigour to the Missionary Movement. That is not to say that without Christianity it is impossible to attain a full spiritual life; very many "good" people do so. How do we reconcile the non-Christian but spiritual quality of, say, Socrates, Marcus Aurelius, Confucius or Ghandi with the simple Christian faith of Mrs Bloggs who supports her church devotedly but seems to have achieved nothing in life? "By their fruits ye shall know them" (Matt. Ch. 7, 20). Is this an adequate answer?

I do not know how to answer this question. Perhaps it requires no better answer than St John (Ch. 14, 2): "In my Father's House are many mansions, if it were not so I would have told you". I choose to believe in Jesus Christ; but I do not believe this means that I should try to enforce my own beliefs on others of mature spirituality who have reached this state along a different path. Religious curiosity is a delicate plant and has to germinate in its own peculiar way, often from something that seems trivial, or sometimes from the example, perceived by indifferent people, of the life-pattern of known Christians.

If curiosity must come first, competent and convincing explanation has to follow; for this reason Christian people, especially those accepted as leaders, must be ready to answer questions, and try to explain WHY...Only as a result of sensible, gentle and attractive answers should anyone be expected to accept Jesus as Lord and to commit themselves to follow Him. Today, it is not enough just to proclaim, "Christ is Risen". We live in an educated, sceptical, and prosperous age, and religious curiosity must be met by sensible, intelligible answers. Commitment may not be immediate; deep heart-searching is often necessary first. These stages of religious conversion bear no resemblance to passing an examination in religious knowledge; but they certainly resemble the pattern of 'falling in love'.

Conversion Experiences from the Past.

It seems appropriate at this stage very briefly to take note of some 'conversion experiences' from the past which are on record in the *Encyclopaedia Britannica:*

"St Augustine was fashionably brought up and had a Christian mother. In early adult life he was under spiritual stress with intellectual difficulties. He came under the influence of Ambrose of Milan which culminated in his baptism three years later in 387 AD.

St Benedict (480-544 AD) was shocked in early adult life by the prevailing licentiousness. It led him to become a recluse for three years; then disciples flocked to him and he founded a monastic order.

St Gregory the First was the son of wealthy Roman parents and became Prefect of Rome. At the age of 33, in 574 AD he felt irresistibly attracted to a religious life, entered a Benedictine monastery, later becoming Pope.

Ignatius Loyola was the youngest son of a Spanish nobleman who chose a military career. During convalescence after being wounded, a vivid conversion led to a strict life and the founding of the Jesuit movement in 1540.

Teresa of Avila came from a comfortably-off family and enjoyed the pleasures of life, but she was afraid of marriage, perhaps because her mother died in childbirth. Reluctantly, in 1533 she entered a Carmelite convent (respectable young women had little choice but marriage or the veil). Twenty years later she wrote: "I could not possibly doubt that the Lord was within me and I in Him". She founded other convents, and led a conspicuously compassionate life.[4]"

One could quote many other conversions, but such vivid experiences are not common among millions of Christian people at the periphery, many of whom are not even baptised, but would certainly wish to be counted as Christian adherents - and why not? *Christianity is not the private possession of an exclusive society.*

At the opposite extreme, a far smaller number of lovely people have been reared in deeply sincere Christian families and have never encountered the *'Vanity Fairs'* of this life. Their unchallenged (but Christian) beliefs guide them successfully through a placid and circumscribed life.

The temperament, intellect, upbringing and status of men and women apply just as much to Christians as to others.

References.

1. William Sargant *Battle for the Mind* (Heinemann) 1957
2. C.G. Jung *Modern Man in Search of a Soul* (Kegan Paul) 1936. p.261
3. E.W. Barnes *Rise of Christianity* (Longman, Green & Co. 1947. p.337
4. *Encyclopaedia Britannica* (14th Ed)

St Paul and Some of His Problems

Personal Background.

The importance of St Paul to Christianity is twofold.

Firstly, his Epistles comprise the earliest writings in the New Testament.

Secondly, by his missionary zeal, he more than anyone was instrumental in the early spreading of Christianity, particularly to some major cities in the Roman Empire.

St Paul was a very tough traveller, and he must have been of very strong physique. When the Holy Spirit forbad him and his companions entry to Bithynia (Acts Ch. 16, 7-8), "they, passing by Mysia, came down to Troas". On a later occasion, while his friends sailed from Troas round Cape Baba to Assos, St Paul walked the thirty miles over difficult terrain to meet them there. Despite imprisonments and tortures, at the age of about sixty he apparently walked from Naples to Rome. John Pollock, [1.] in *The Apostle* gives considerable detail regarding the difficulties and dangers of travel arrangements for an ordinary person in those days.

Tent-making was the traditional local trade in Tarsus where Luke says St Paul was born probably about 1 AD (Acts Ch. 22, 3). According to Luke, St Paul himself claimed to have learned the Jewish law from Gamaliel in Jerusalem, and thus to have become a Pharisee and a Rabbi. St Paul belonged to the Jewish tribe of Benjamin which, according to Hugh Montefiore,[2] put him in good standing as a Jew. He was also a Roman citizen. In his day such status, Montefiore suggests, was probably rather like a royal birthday honour bestowed on some worthy person.[3] It carried certain civil privileges. Thus it is probably fair to say that St Paul was of artisan or middle class rather than rural peasant background, and certainly better educated than the Lord's disciples from Galilee.

St Paul's Conversion.

This is often described and accepted as a miraculous event - but what is a miracle? How did Saul, the Pharisee, 'convert' to become St Paul, the Christian? At first scrutiny his conversion seems not to follow the four stages of the Emmaus Road story! Saul the Pharisee had been fanatical in persecuting the Christians in Jerusalem.With the backing of Sanhedrin he then stormed off to persecute the Christians similarly in Damascus. That journey (about 120 miles) could not have been easily accomplished in one day and, depending on available resources, probably took several days.

Thus, "as he came near Damascus" (Acts Ch. 9, 3), Saul must have had plenty of time for reflection while he travelled (leading to curiosity or doubt?). Then, rather than Jesus "walking with him", as on the Emmaus Road, Saul heard an unrecognised voice (explanation?). He "trembled and was astonished" (emotion), and was told to "arise and go ..." Then he was three days "without sight" until Ananias, albeit rather reluctantly, "put hands on him" and Paul received sight forthwith (acceptance), (Acts Ch. 9, 18) and was baptised (commitment). I think that careful consideration of the famous Damascus Road conversion does accord with the four stages of conversion that I have suggested in the Emmaus Road story: (curiosity, explanation, acceptance, commitment). From that moment, Paul was as convinced a disciple of Jesus as were the other disciples who, by Lake Galilee, responded to the call: "Follow me". Whether or not the Damascus Road story was the first recorded Christian conversion of anyone who had not known Jesus of Nazareth during His lifetime, it was certainly the most significant for history. Paul himself insisted that it was just as valid a conversion as that experienced by those who had known Jesus of Nazareth himself (Gal Ch. 1, 12).

All such conversions as happened to St Paul inevitably raise important difficulties. Does it necessarily follow that if one person can receive the Gospel message by such direct revelation, other persons can too? More importantly: will such revelations to different persons be similar? Will the conversions of different persons by such direct revelation have the same significance for all of them? If so, will their different accounts of their individual experiences from such personal revelations be equally valid?

As will be seen later, it is just such searching questions as these that have inevitably perplexed and troubled the Christian Church throughout the centuries, and continue to do so to the present day. I do not think that mankind knows how to accommodate such ways of thought because they are so very individual and concern every man's relationship to God.

St Paul's Missionary Programme.

We can only surmise the possible reasons that led St Paul to choose the routes for his journeys; they seem to progress from one large town to another, and usually by the established and safest routes. Why did the Holy Spirit not suffer them to go into Bithynia? (Acts Ch. 16, 7). In the linguistic style of those times it may have corresponded to our being advised against driving directly through the mountains from Hieropolis to Philadelphia, but rather to take the longer coastal route. A kindly inn-keeper simply advised us that the mountain people did not welcome strangers. We took the hint! Maybe St Paul did likewise?

When St Paul reached a city he usually sought to teach in the Jewish synagogue as a Rabbi, but was usually thrown out sooner or later for preaching Christianity rather than Judaism - which is certainly understandable because it disturbed the local Jewish communities. It seems to me that this Pauline experience was very similar to the way people in Jerusalem had felt disturbed by Jesus, and which finally led to His crucifixion.

SUCH REJECTION IS THE USUAL CORPORATE BEHAVIOURAL REACTION OF ORDINARY PEOPLE WHO FEEL THREATENED BY NEW IDEAS THAT THEY DO NOT WISH TO ASSIMILATE.

As the provincial synagogues progressively rejected Paul's Christian teaching (eg Philippi, Salonika, Verria, Athens, Ephesus), so a few of their people *did* accept him; and this led to the establishment of tiny new Christian communities.Today we know of these from the Epistles St Paul later wrote to them, often to 'iron-out' their different problems.

Biblical Criticism and St Paul's Epistles.

What were these problems that led to Paul's rejection by the synagogues? Can we discover them today? Professor Hodgson has expressed this question succinctly: "What must the truth be, and have been, if it appeared like that to men who thought and wrote as they did?" [4.] The Jewish rite of circumcision was certainly one big issue for sincere Jews. Also, to some extent, the next chapter offers clues about contemporary difficulties in St Paul's writing to the Roman Christians.

Until as recently as the nineteenth century St Paul's Epistles were widely assumed to be elaborate theological writings. However, modern biblical criticism has realised that they are indeed letters in the manner of those times: not so much personal letters from one man to a friend, but rather the sort of open letter that someone might write to a newspaper today to spread information more widely. Historical and redaction criticism, together with archaeological and literary research, now enable us to know more about St Paul than ever before.

As Christianity spread into Europe and Asia Minor - and St Paul was its greatest missionary pioneer - it was undoubtedly influenced by other religious thought and practice. E.W. Barnes writes: "As Christianity made its way over the Mediterranean area in the century following the death of its Lord, it did not escape the process of change...

It has often been said that Christianity ultimately triumphed in the ancient world as a mystery religion; and undoubtedly the influence of ideas from these faiths is to be found in the New Testament, especially in the writings attributed to St Paul".[5.]

Thus, we have to acknowledge that, whereas Jesus expressed his profound insights and unique teaching within the context of Judaism, St Paul, extending more widely those marvellous insights and teaching which are absolutely central to Christianity, succeeded in transmitting them in a form which was acceptable to Hellenistic populations (Greeks), while at the same time preserving the original Jewish framework in which they had originally been expressed by Jesus himself. It is because of Paul's more expansive interpretation of Christianity that it survived in Europe while, seen only as a Jewish sect in the Middle East, it did not.

The Mystery Religions in St Paul's Time.

The mystery religions of the first century differed from the official Roman or Greek state religion in that the state religion was public, while the mystery religions involved secret rituals. The different mystery religions had certain prominent features in common. The Official Gods of both Rome and Greece flitted in and out of the world, while the God(s) of these "societies" remained transcendental (ie their existence was deemed to be wholly apart from the material world). Also, these Gods of the mystery religions were inclined to scorn the fleshly delightsof this world. W.R. Inge, sometime Dean of St Paul's Cathedral,

London, has further emphasised the secrecy that was attached to their different ceremonies and rituals and which were held to be an indispensable means of redemption for the attainment of individual immortality.[6]

Very early Christianity was regarded as a mystery religion by most outsiders. Among Jewish converts to Christianity the background was obviously Judaic; but among non-Jewish converts it was a mystery religion. In England today, C of E is the state religion, but there exists alongside it the complete freedom of other Christian denominations, or even entirely different religious beliefs.

The Judaic carry-over into Christianity is acknowledged and incorporated into the Christian Bible as its Old Testament. In this way, its deep religious insights and values are recognised and appreciated by Christian people.

The basis of those mystery faiths at the beginning of the Christian era was the idea of the renewal of life, especially as we see it every springtime. It was not irrelevant, therefore, to ask: can mankind similarly live a renewed life after apparent death? This question goes back at least several thousand years into man's primitive religious history (magical animism). However, at the time of Jesus Christ and St Paul, Mithraism and Orphism were probably the most influential religions of this type.[5]

Orphism had existed in Greece for at least five hundred years or more, gradually discarding its more repulsive and barbaric aspects. This cult held Dionysus as a God of fruitfulness, and taught the salvation of the 'individual soul' (a Greek concept) through various kinds of religious ceremonies and orgies. These apparently moderated and gave rise to the Eleusinian mysteries, which persisted for over a thousand years, centering on the sight and handling of Holy Things, which constituted a ritual associated with some sort of assurance of immortality. The notable philosopher Pythagoras was associated with this religion.

Mithra was the Zoroastrian God of fruitfulness, whose cult (though dating from perhaps 800 BC in Persia) apparently reached Rome not earlier than about 60 BC.[5.] A God of light, he was therefore in opposition to darkness - a defender of truth against evil. The bull was symbolic of evil and Mithra overcame it, although he found the slaying of the bull repugnant. His various tasks on earth completed, Mithra apparently ascended to heaven to watch and to succour his followers. There is evidence that at the end of the second century AD Mithraism may have been more widespread than Christianity, particularly among Roman soldiery, and this may be why the Roman Emperor Julian the Apostate tried to make it the official Roman religion.

The Mithraic rites and Christianity both tended to copy ideas and rituals from each other.[5, 6, 7, 8.] In the end the more pacifist Christian Church triumphed over the more popular soldiers' religion, the risen Christ over the venerated god of light.

This religious outcome, although spread over two or three centuries, seems quite inexplicable in a world so swayed by superstition.

References.

1. Pollock, J. *The Apostle* (Hodder and Stoughton), 1969
2. Montefiore, H. *Paul the Apostle* (Collins), 1981, p.16
3. Montefiore, H. op. cit. p.17
4. Lampe, G.W.H. *Christian Believing* (S.P.C.K.), 1976, p.101
5. Barnes, E.W. *Rise of Christianity* (Longmans Green & Co), 1947
6. Inge, W.R. *Outspoken Essays* (Longmans Green & Co), 1924
7. *Everyman's Encyclopaedia* (Dent), 1913
8. *Encyclopaedia Britannica* 14th Ed., 1929

St Paul's Epistle to The Romans

St Augustine, aged 33 in 386 AD, was sitting in the garden, distressed, when he read Chapter 13 of "Romans". It provided the "explanation" he needed for his conversion, and he became the pre-eminent Christian leader of his time.

In 1498-9, Erasmus visited Oxford and heard John Colet's humanist lecture on St Paul's personality and the Epistle to the Romans, which influenced his theological writing in the following decades.

Martin Luther was an academic Augustinian monk, and was greatly perplexed by the very secular ecclesiasticism he had found in Rome on a visit there in 1510 (doubt or curiosity?). During the winter of 1512-13, his mind suddenly cleared while meditating on Romans Ch. 1, 16-17 (explanation or acceptance). He then wrote a series of lectures on Romans, and three years later on Oct. 31st, 1517, he nailed his epoch-making challenge to the door of the Church in Wittenberg (commitment).

John Wesley, in a state of spiritual uncertainty for several months after returning from Georgia, had been reading Luther's preface to "Romans" (explanation) just before "his heart was strangely warmed" in Aldersgate on May 24th, 1738 (acceptance). Methodism began at a love-feast held on Jan. 1st, 1739 (commitment).

It is obviously necessary to try to discover the meaning of a tract that has had such immense influence on four such remarkable men, spread over a thousand years of Christianity. This very great exposition of Christianity by St Paul is the nearest we have to the setting out of his own 'Credo' as a theological treatise for posterity, in contrast to his other letters, which were usually based to some extent on his advice or ruling concerning a local problem, because in those days each of the small, separate Christian communities tended still to be dependent on the teaching of their founder.

The Epistle to the Romans was probably dictated in Corinth in 55 or 56 AD and Paul sets out his own beliefs to introduce himself to the Christians of Rome. He had never been to Rome when he wrote this letter; someone else had founded the earliest Christian community there, but Paul was hoping to go there soon. The content of the Epistle divides conveniently into three parts: the first eight chapters are concerned with Mankind's relationship to God. Then three chapters concern the 'predicament' of the Jews. Really, this is Paul's own predicament, his having been rejected by so many different Synagogues. The Epistle concludes with a section from chapter twelve onwards, which is concerned with Christian behaviour.

This Epistle is by no means easy to understand! Firstly, the translation from Greek is difficult, and translators are not unanimous regarding its meaning and the nuances of its language. Secondly, knowledge of the world generally at the time in which Paul lived was so very different from our own understanding of the world today. Thirdly, a number of "ideas" which Paul could take for granted, we do not: for instance, slavery, demons, evil, or sin and death, because as time has passed, the significance of those and other terms has changed. Finally, it is not easy for us to remember that in his time, there was no generally accepted body of Christian doctrine, no accepted Christian creed and no sort of agreed form of orthodox Christianity.

Chapters 1 - 4: Justification by Faith.

In the approved style of the time Paul opens with a flamboyant address, culminating in the phrase that so impressed Luther: "The Just shall live by Faith" (Ch. 1, 17). But Paul embarks immediately on a long digression about the wrath of God: "The soul that sinneth it shall surely die" (c.f. Ez., Ch. 18, 20 and c.f. Rom. Ch. 6, 23). This lengthy statement about wrath seems out of place, but even so it is an important religious insight. Paul is rightly concerned to establish early on that we break God's law at our own peril, and that to do this leads to suffering as an inevitable consequence (eg nowadays: divorce, abortion, pollution, degradation of inner cities...?). In Paul's day the issues were different, but he makes the point that a breach of God's moral law is a form of selfishness; ie that the root of sin is disobedience.

He resumes his main argument in Ch. 3, 21 to establish how one may achieve this right relationship with God, ie *salvation*. In modern parlance, Paul is saying that "Brother, are you saved?" *means* "In your inmost heart have you attained a right relationship with your understanding of God?" This is a relationship that cannot be attained by hard work (such as writing this book!). It requires faith. I find this word "faith" an unsatisfactory and vague term: it is not a command to believe something impossible, but to back an inspired guess which may turn out to be correct. (eg. I have faith that someone may actually read this book!) For Paul, faith implied more than loyalty: It meant a profound conviction that something is true, even when that "something" cannot possibly be proved by logical thought. It is impossible to 'prove' the beauty of the view from a high mountain at dawn on a clear day; it is impossible to 'prove' the emotional effect of the fourth movement of Beethoven's fifth symphony; or that Mount Everest exists if you haven't seen it! But, if you have contemplated the view from a rustic hillock, then by faith you may be able to accept that the perspective in the High Alps is wonderful; if you have felt moved by the singing of "Rule Britannia" you may be able to accept that there can be depths of emotional response to Beethoven; and if you have never seen Mount Everest there is an element of faith if you are prepared to believe others who say that it is really there! For Paul, faith is something like this: total acceptance and trust that there is a God, and assent to the consequences.

Chapters 5 - 8: Further Difficulties.

Having established that we can obtain a right relationship with God by faith in Jesus Christ, does this mean that afterwards we may behave just as we choose? If forgiveness for earlier sin is attainable, are we then at liberty to disregard the Jewish "Law"? And if we can sort out *sin* - then what about *death?*

Today we do not readily associate sin with death. The ancient belief of primitive mankind was that sin *was* a cause of death! Therefore, Paul asks, even if God is willing to forgive the man who has *sinned,* will that man nevertheless *die?* (In Magical Animism there was widespread belief that life was perpetual (the Garden of Eden) unless terminated by the Gods, or by sorcery, or by accident.) So, if God would accept the sinner despite his sin, then what about his life? Would he be "let off" death? The contemporary rituals of Mithraism and other mystery religions claimed that they could enable a man to win some kind of perpetual life.

Paul tries to argue a relationship between the sin of ancient Adam in Genesis, and the redeeming power of Christ (because in Paul's thought, Adam and Christ are inextricably linked!). C.K. Barrett [1.] W. Barclay [2.] and H. Montefiore [3.] all admit that the argument is difficult to understand. I must confess that I find his argument unconvincing. Certainly a man can be ruined by sin and yet rescued by the grace of God, but I do not see any need to invoke the mythology of Genesis to explain this.

Nevertheless, Justification by Faith (ie attaining a right relationship with God), does *not mean* that we can behave irresponsibly afterwards. Paul rebuts the idea of such trading on the mercy of God and emphasises that the man who enters on the Christian way of life by baptism commits himself to a new way of life (ie he is born again).

Paul then reverts to the interesting metaphor of slavery. The feudal system, so interwoven with Christianity in the middle ages, probably began to take shape in Roman times, but slavery is far more ancient. Paul argues that by becoming "a slave to God" through the mediation of Jesus Christ, one was no longer a "slave" to sin (ie the

Evil Power). Paul had a very different concept of freedom from that which prevails today; he accepted that men must always be slaves to either a good master or a bad one. [4, 5] This makes it clearer to us how the sacrifice of Jesus as a ransom could be understood (see p. 29); with his death, Jesus, so to speak, paid a cash price for the Christians, who thereby became His possessions.Our contemporary ideas of freedom or human rights were not known to Paul. According to Paul, man is never "born free but is everywhere in chains" (Rousseau). Paul believed that it is in the very nature of society that man is always a slave, and never free. [6]

In chapter seven, Paul considers the relationship of sin and "Law" ("Law" in this context being the whole of O.T. religion), and he asks: If a man is rescued by Christ from sin and if a man is rescued by Christ from the Law, then what is the difference between sin and the Law? Paul points out that sometimes when there is a Law one becomes aware of an interest in breaking it; the Law enhances awareness of sin, and the greater one's esteem for the Law, the greater one's dejection from sin. Paul reaches the conclusion that since Justification by Faith can overcome sin, all men will die in the flesh, but that the man whose whole life is controlled by the Holy Spirit (ie enslaved to God) will rise again: "For I reckon that the sufferings of the present time are not worthy to be compared with the glory which shall be revealed in us" (Ch. 8, 18).

It is important to realise that these difficult Pauline concepts were not merely very meaningful to him, but that he had had to rethink his beliefs in relation to his own Christ-experience. Although Paul certainly believed that Jesus was the Messiah - as proved by His Resurrection - His Resurrection nevertheless leaves a gap, because the Messiah is meant to usher in a New World (of some sort!). Because this New World has not yet arrived, Paul is convinced that Jesus is going to return to this world in glory to set it up! This is quite a different Messianic hope from that of the Maccabean revolt a couple of centuries earlier, but Paul undoubtedly believed that the coming of "The Kingdom of God" was imminent, probably within his own life-time. This was also the widespread belief and longing of the earliest Christian Church.

With the ejection of Christians from the synagogues, and the passing of centuries, the later Christian Church has inevitably modified the doctrines which arise from this early belief of our Christian forefathers, and today it seems hardly possible for an intelligent person to accept St Paul's beliefs about the future life of the individual or the destiny of the world.

However, it was Paul who coined the lovely simile of the redeemed Christian being brought by adoption into the family of God (Ch. 8, 14 & 15) and declared the love of God for His family. Paul goes on to state the assurance that if God accepts us, hopeless creatures though we are, nothing else can matter!

The paean of joy and confidence in such poetic language as ends chapter eight, is in no way diminished by the knowledge that its ideas are untenable in mere physical terms. St Paul is proclaiming an eternal truth in the language and thought pictures of his time.

Chapters 9 - 11. The Problem of the Jews.

Paul reflects on his difficulty as a Jewish Rabbi, preaching Christianity to both Jew and Gentile alike, which certainly troubled him deeply: If the Jews were God's Chosen People (thought Paul) *how* could they possibly reject Jesus as their Messiah? After much heart-searching he concludes that the *whole* of the Jewish race *never was* the Chosen People, but only a "righteous remnant" who were selected by God! He argues that God is exercising His divine prerogative which it is not for Man to question!

This is the origin of the strange doctrine of predestination: God had "chosen" Isaac but not Ishmael; Jacob but not Esau. In consequence, this argument has been used repeatedly to indicate that God has predestined certain men for perdition and others for eternal bliss (Ch. 11, 5). Paul concludes this section with a great acclamation in Chapter 11, 33-36.

Chapters 12 -15. Christian Behaviour.

Paul, therefore, having wrestled with the problems of the Risen Messiah, rejected by his Chosen People yet commendable to the Gentiles, must declare the pattern of life that is implicit in the acceptance of Jesus as Lord. This he does.

The Epistle concludes with Paul endeavouring to explain how Jews *should* understand the "Law", to express the spirit and meaning of it in their conduct, rather than as a formal and unfeeling obedience to mere rules. He points out that the ethical expression of the true meaning of the law, *when rightly understood,* expresses itself in "love" (Ch. 13, 10). The *Law of Christ* is not just a means to salvation, but the ethical channel through which the new life in Christ flows.[7]

He reiterates that men are not justified and reconciled to God by vegetarianism, or sabbatarianism, by teetotalism or any other abstentions, but by faith alone and God's grace.[8] Even in the Church today, as Paul recognised long ago (Ch. 14, 1), there are stronger and weaker brethren, and Paul admonishes those who think themselves stronger to do nothing that will embarrass those who seem weaker. We would do well to remember that in many matters it is our duty to hold our own convictions, but to allow others to differ without regarding them as sinners and outcasts.

This whole section - indeed *all the Pauline writing* - has to be understood within the framework of Paul's convictions about the ultimate destiny of this world (Ch. 13, 11 - 13). He declares that since the death and resurrection of Jesus, "this age" can no longer be the regulative principle of life for those who have "died and been raised" (converted). Pending the second coming of Christ in Glory, the pattern of behaviour he lays down is essential. Christian behaviour only arises out of Christian belief and obedience to it; but Christian people need guidance as to how that obedience should be seen in their behaviour.

It is important for Paul to teach and show the moral significance and real meaning of the Old Testament Jewish law. It is essential for the modern reader to realise and respect Paul's own beliefs about the ultimate destiny of this world, because this gives added power and authority to all his teaching. It is also important to realise that he proclaimed Jesus Christ offers *salvation* to all men, and that the Church must welcome all men - *the Church can never be an exclusive society (Ch. 10, 11 - 14).*

References.

1. Barrett, C.K. *A Commentary on the Epistle to the Romans* (Black) 1957, p.110
2. Barclay, W. *The Letter to the Romans* (St Andrews Press) 1955, p.77
3. Montefiore, H. *Paul the Apostle* (Collins) 1981, p.76
4. Barrett, C.K. op. cit. p.132
5. Kummel *The theology of the New Testament* (S.C.M. Press) 1974, p.158
6. Kummel op. cit. p.187
7. Barrett op. cit. p.251
8. Barrett op. cit. p.256

An Unusual Dream

It must be more than twenty years since I saw the statue.* I was walking down a side-street near Notting Hill Gate, and there it was on the other side of the road. I crossed to look more closely, because there were two lambs at his feet, and he was dressed to resemble a cardinal. But I noticed the church behind him was a plain unattractive building; in fact a nineteenth century Baptist Chapel. I noticed that below the statue of the cleric was a plaque that read:

"To commemorate the Christian efforts of the Originators of Sunday Schools from Cardinal Borromeo in 1580 to Robert Raikes in 1780, IN FERVENT HOPE THAT THE TIME MAY SOON COME WHEN DIFFERENCES OF OPINION WILL NO LONGER SEPARATE THE DISCIPLES OF CHRIST IN WORKS OF USEFULNESS."

Isn't that fascinating! A cardinal outside a Baptist Chapel in honour of an Anglican, and put there a hundred years ago!

I was so surprised, and thought how very *avant garde* that was for those old-time people. Just at that moment I was stopped by a tap on the arm from a rather bow-legged little man with a badly scarred face. In a beautifully gentle and musical voice he asked me if I could

* It was about 1968 when I did actually see the statue (near Palace Gardens off Bayswater Road). I returned some months later, but it had been removed.

explain to him the meaning of an inscription on a building that he had just passed which indicated that it was METHODIST. So I said, "Oh yes, those people are followers of John and Charles Wesley who revived Christianity in England 250 years ago," to which he replied, "I heard some singing from inside as I passed by." I said that wasn't very surprising, because Methodism was born in song, and they sang some very fine hymns. "But excuse me," I said, "What are you doing here, why do you ask me these things?" "Well, as a matter of fact, I just dropped in while I was passing, to look at the gracious building on the other side of the city which bears my name, although I have never come as far as this before. I have just walked over here, admiring the spacious beauty of this town." I thought that sounded a bit odd, and I wondered who on earth he was, and even whether he had escaped from a mental hospital! He perceived my uncertainty, and went on: "My name is Paul, but I believe you speak of me nowadays as St Paul. But", he continued, "do you understand why this building has the word BAPTIST inscribed on it?" "Yes sir," I said, "these are good people who serve a very useful purpose by their emphasis on Baptism."

"I saw another church on my way," the man continued, "and a passer-by told me that it was ROMAN, but it did not look very old, can you explain that?" "Yes, I think I can, Sir," I said. "That is a very great church indeed because it originated from the missionary work that you and St Peter did together in Rome; and ever since those days the Head of that Church has always been regarded as the direct successor of St Peter as Bishop of Rome."

"That is a kind allusion to our ministry, although I must admit I always found him rather difficult to get on with," smiled the man. "Peter was inclined to be impetuous, but he was fond of fishing, and he never liked travelling much. But I saw another church still, that was called the Church of England, down by the river; I think the district was called Westminster. Would that have something to do with Peter?" "I suppose it might," I said hesitantly, "because it does say somewhere inside that it was built to the honour of God and St Peter." "Then if it commemorates St Peter, why do you call it the 'Church of England'?" I began to feel slightly uncomfortable. I remembered that St Paul probably knew far more law than I ever did, and I perceived that he had a lively curiosity. "The Church of England", I said, "differs from the Church of Rome in that the Head of it is Sovereign of this country, the Queen, and she has appointed bishops, and through them priests, to serve every part of our country in areas called parishes, so that no matter where one lives there will always be a parish priest to minister to each one of us." I hoped this would satisfy him!

"That sounds a good idea," commented this friendly saint, "but tell me - because I used to sing a lot in times of trouble - do *only* the Methodists sing to the praise of God?" "Oh no, your Lordship, all the Churches sing to the praise of God, and some sing very beautifully."

"You mentioned the Baptists," he went on, "Do any other churches baptise?" "Yes, your Grace," I answered, not being sure how one should address a real saint. "All the churches we have mentioned certainly try to baptise their members." "What do you mean 'try to baptise?" he retorted."Well, I don't know exactly why, but certainly not all the people who come to worship are baptised," I answered, feeling uncomfortably that it might be my fault! "Do the people in these churches all acknowledge that Jesus Christ is our Lord and Master?" "I'm sure they do," I answered."Very well, in that case, which of these churches do you yourself belong to, and how do you choose which one to support?" Suddenly, as often happens when dreams become difficult, I woke up!!

This might have happened to you one restless night; in that case, I wonder, how would you have explained these differences to St Paul, and the reasons for your choice?

Four Christian Enigmas

Love, Evil, Suffering, Fear.

Love, together with Evil and Suffering and Fear, are among the very profound issues which every man and woman must expect to encounter at various times on his or her journey through life.

We must be prepared to meet each of them unexpectedly at some time on life's pilgrimage: perhaps in childhood, then in adolescence and again in the different stages of adult life.How we come to terms with them moulds our character, and whether we realise this or not, how we come to terms with each one also depends very much on our religious outlook.

I state my own beliefs about these matters; I hope they may help others to work out theirs.

Love

Christianity is much more like "falling in love" than being top of the Religious Education class at school! There are aspects of life that we try to explain in words, although we all know that words are not adequate. Metaphors from the beauty of a mountain view, and the harmony of great music have already been mentioned. One might similarly refer to the human spirit being moved by great paintings: there is the story of the visitor to the Louvre who went round the galleries in ten minutes and told the concierge as he left that he didn't think much of the pictures.To which the concierge is supposed to have replied, "The pictures, sir, are not on trial but you are!" Christianity is also a bit like that.

Sir William Rees-Mogg, a former editor of *The Times*, has written: "The strongest evidence of the truth of God's Love, of the existence of God and the existence of his Love, is not to be found in philosophy, but in the working of God's Love that can be seen in the lives of men. Not all good men are religious, but there is a large group of men of whom examples can be found in all ages, and all countries, and all religions. They show a freedom from normal selfishness and a capacity for love which human nature only shows at its highest. They all say, in different theological terms, that they have received this blessing from God." [1.]

The historian, Arthur Bryant, declared that it was Christ's unique achievement that he alone of the great teachers in history taught that the Kingdom of God resides in every heart, and that God is Love.[2]

Long, long ago, in words attributed to St John, someone else wrote:

"Love is of God...for God is Love".

How can God possibly *be* Love? It does seem to call for a bit of 'topsy-turvy' thinking, but the thought may not be so ridiculous as it first appears. The idea of an anthropomorphic God with a long beard sitting on the heavenly throne is simply a medieval, man-made artistic idea. No man can know, first-hand, what God is like; that would be like a spade wondering about the plans in the mind of a landscape gardener - even though a spade may be the essential tool for putting those landscape ideas into practice.

The real nature of God must be beyond the comprehension of man. At best we can only perceive the outcome of the energies of God: the majesty of the Universe, The Wonder of living things, the Personalities of men and women. The Love that is of God must surely be of boundless dimension, utterly transcending the possibility of any human understanding. Therefore making every allowance for the shortcomings of language and the inadequacy of mere words, it is not unreasonable to admit that God may be Love. It is not unreasonable to acknowledge that this is at least an admissible hypothesis!

The Christian simply concedes, in blind trust, that the nearest we can come to understanding the essence of God, in human terms, is through its expression in Jesus Christ.

What Do We Mean by 'Love'?

We do need to clear our thoughts about the real meaning of this word 'Love'. There are more 'pop' songs about love than about any other subject; youths and maidens spend much time declaring their mutual love - they always have done; but is that what we mean by the Love of God?

Our English word 'love' is used to translate four different words from the language of our New Testament. Very often we have to cross a language barrier to avoid being confused by the words used two thousand years ago. 'Eros', 'Storge', 'Philia' and 'Agape' are all translated into English as 'Love'.

Eros means love in its passionate, sexual sense; Storge signifies love in its domestic, family or tribal sense; Philia means the love of ideas and reason so richly esteemed by the great Greek thinkers; and Agape is often translated loosely as 'compassion'.

Sex, family, ideas and compassion: all wonderful gifts from God, and all these meanings to be found in the one English word 'love'! Is it stretching linguistic imagination too far to suggest that in the sacrament of marriage we can recognise the holiness of sex; in the sacrament of baptism we can perceive the holiness of family; in the sacrament of ordination we can discern the holiness of understanding; and that in the Eucharist we can accept the holiness of compassion? May not all these be just different expressions, however dimly we perceive them, of the Love of God?

Jesus' Teaching on Love.

Jesus declares that we must love the Lord our God with our heart, soul and mind, ***and*** also our neighbour as ourself (Lk Ch. 10, 27 & 28). This is where it starts to become difficult; like the devout, white English lady who supported foreign missions for the conversion of black people, but recoiled in dismay when a real negro bought the house next door and became her genuine physical neighbour!

Jesus teaches that I am to express the love of God by the yardstick of the love that I show toward my neighbour; and my neighbour is anyone who needs me, needs help that I am able to give, here and now; perhaps someone I cherish dearly, but perhaps sometimes a complete stranger.

That is the meaning of the marvellous story Jesus tells about the man who fell among thieves on the road to Jerico! (Lk Ch. 10, 25ff.)

Neighbourliness lays on each of us an immense responsibility of service to our fellow men and women, which has nothing to do with whether we know them or like them. And it is loving service that we are constrained to give, not a grudging minimal degree of help. That is what Christianity is all about.

Such are the constraints of love if we can commit ourselves to such discipline. That is why I had to begin this chapter by saying that this term 'Love' goes beyond the capacity of language. It also goes a long way beyond the Will and the Strength and the Stamina of most of us. But when you 'fall in love' you stop counting the cost in yardstick terms.

In Jesus Christ we discover that this is what real living is all about:it is 'falling in love' with life at its richest and best.

This way of life does indeed bring gentleness, peace and joy (Gal. Ch. 5, 22); but Love is a vigorous and turbulent force as well, and it calls for discipline, renunciation and forgiveness. Love does "bear all things" and Love does "endure all things" (1 Cor. Ch. 13, 7).

At the end of His life Jesus stated this perfectly clearly: "This is my commandment, that ye love one another as I have loved you." (John, Ch. 15, v. 12)

St Paul wrote to the Ephesians (Ch. 3, 17ff): "And I pray that Christ will be more and more at home in your hearts, living within you as you trust in Him. May your roots go down deep into the soil of God's marvellous love; and may you be able to feel and understand, as all God's children should, how long, how wide, how deep and how high His love really is; and to experience this love for yourselves though it is so great that you will never see the end of it or fully know or understand it. And so at last you will be filled up with God himself.."[3.]

References.

1. W. Rees-Mogg *An Humbler Heaven* (Hamish Hamilton), 1977, p.17-18

2. A. Bryant *The Lion and the Unicorn* (Collins), 1969, p.339

3. *The Living Bible*. (Coverdale House), 1974.

Evil

It has often been said that the toughest problem with which Christians have to come to terms is that of Evil.

"Why does God (if there is a God?) allow ***It*** *to happen?"* is a world-wide response to all kinds of tragedy, and if Christianity has any real strength and meaning (which it certainly claims), it must be able to respond constructively to the many unfortunate events that we see and hear of every day, both in our own experience and through modern media communication. Many people have turned away from Christianity, and from religion generally (that is, as *they* understand religion) because they have failed to discover any satisfactory religious response to tragedy. "Why does God let it happen?" leads them only too rapidly to the wrong conclusion. They conclude: "Because there is no God and no purpose in life" - instead of tackling the more profound proposition: "How can an all powerful God be Love, if tragedy, wickedness and suffering exist so extensively around us?"

A Possible Origin of Evil.

We need to enquire further into how mankind has arrived at these concepts of good and evil. Let it be supposed that *homo sapiens* so evolved as to appear on this planet sometime about 50,000 years or more ago - which is a plausible supposition. Let us keep this perspective of mankind on an anthropological time scale; this often helps to maintain our proper sense of humility! After all, we can accept that a trapeze act requires much practice and that there may sometimes be accidents; or that a fine performance of, say, a Shakespeare play requires time and effort in preparation and rehearsal before the show. There is no obvious reason why the development of mankind should be different. We know virtually nothing of his thought, religion or behaviour until the curtain rises, perhaps about 10,000 years ago when he was beginning to become *homo religiosus.* Mankind certainly has innate curiosity, and the myths in the early chapters of *Genesis* express some of ancient mankind's conjectures about creation and the events at that time.

He was repeatedly confounded by, for instance, storm, or flood, or disease, and so it is perhaps from such experiences that he first responded by developing the concept of local gods, whom he believed had greater power than he possessed and who could (sometimes) influence those mighty phenomena which he could not control. Only from then can such matters as Right and Wrong, Good and Evil, Gods and Demons, Heaven and Hell enter human thought. It is relatively a very small part indeed of the time-scale in terms of the whole Creation. That does not mean that it is an unimportant part. There is no reason to suppose that Creation in all its tremendous magnificence has unfolded smoothly, gradually, at a constant steady pace. Much more probably it has proceeded by mutations and natural selection to an extent that we are only just beginning to realise.

Into this primitive society some sort of regulation had to develop, as is always the case when new organisations emerge in mankind's affairs. Stealing food attracted punishment within the tribe; stealing a man's wife attracted a penalty that began to give meaning to adultery. Thus some of the things a man might do were perceived as "right" while others were "wrong" and attracted punishment by the community. The mere prospect of such penalties added to the fear that came so readily to primitive man, by creating a sense of guilt as well. It thus becomes easier to conjecture that the thought of such possible guilt led to the beginning of conscience.

Religion Relates to Morality.

Because the local gods were by definition more powerful than primitive man, some cultures invoked the wrath of their local gods against offenders. The displeasure of the tribe was appropriately enhanced by the wrath of the appropriate god. Perhaps it was because of confusion from having many local gods that the idea of a "chief god" emerged, leading to monotheism. This development certainly happened in Egypt under Amenhotep in the 14th century BC, and at about this time within Judaism, Moses, too, related morality to the authority of just one god (Ex. Ch. 20). Both these codes of early morality probably derived from the earlier Babylonian Code of Hammurabi (c. 2,000 BC).

Thus we can gain some insight regarding man's earliest concepts of evil and of God. Behaviour that had been morally neutral on the earlier, more animal plane of man's development became immoral as man moved forward on his evolutionary path. If such theories for good and evil are valid, these would seem to link our animal ancestry with the development of human imagination and intelligence, which is in accord with the ideas of modern science. It is important to be clear that such ideas say nothing whatever about the *real* nature of God, nor do they disclose any truth about the existence of evil, apart from man's personal and social involvement, which could be considered as the origin of sin.

In 380 BC Plato wrote in *The Republic:* "God, insomuch as he is good, cannot be the cause of all things, according to the common doctrine. On the contrary, he is the author of only a small part of human affairs; of the largest part he is not the author: for our evil things far outnumber our good things; and the good things we must ascribe to no other than God, while we must seek elsewhere, and not in him, the causes of evil things."[1] This declaration by Plato, although it postulates both a God who is good, and also implies an anti-God as the source of evil (dualism), nevertheless indicates a mighty step upward in man's capacity for religious thought.

However, Judaic religious thought had taken a similar but different step upward several centuries before Plato. The Mosaic Law set out by Moses (c. 1,300 BC) showed that it was advantageous to mankind to insist on some sort of community morality, by which the community, in contrast to individuals or very small groups, became far stronger in resisting "those assaults from the jungle", and which enabled mankind to survive.

A Wider Concept of Christianity.

I believe that the tremendous impact of Jesus Christ

on mankind can usefully be understood in a much wider context, not merely as the most remarkable event of world history, but also as an evolutionary phenomenon to which mankind is still adjusting at an amazing speed.

Ireneus (c. 130-200 AD).

Ireneus [2.] made a contribution to our understanding of good and evil that is not yet widely enough recognised. He lived before the Old Testament hypothesis of the "Fall of Man" (Gen. Ch. 3) was elaborated by St Augustine (in my opinion to a quite unwarranted extent). Ireneus sets out a concept of human affairs that argues a progression from imperfection toward hopes of perfection. Ireneus calls a little child an "Image of God" (Imago), to indicate his nature as an intelligent creature capable of attaining 'fellowship' with his Maker. But this finite creature is as yet only potentially capable of becoming the perfected creature that God is seeking to produce; he is only at the beginning of a process of growth and development in God's continuing providence, which is capable of culminating in the finite likeness of God. Ireneus calls the finished product the "Similitudo".

This concept of an immature individual having the opportunity to progress to maturity is consistent with evolution in enunciating that within God's providence, mankind is somehow or other learning by his contrasting experience of Good and Evil to value the one and to shun the other. Instead of a mankind that was created perfect and which then incomprehensibly destroyed that perfection to plunge into sin and misery, Ireneus suggests that man was created imperfect and immature, but with the opportunity to undergo moral development and growth. In New Testament language he must "be born again". In Scientific language he has the opportunity to "evolve" or develop. Ireneus sees our world of mingled good and evil as a divinely appointed environment for man's development. Rather than a paradise gone wrong, the world is better thought of as similar to a nursery in which a loving parent brings up his children to become the best they are capable of, by exposing them to the hazards of life. Such a parent would not spoil his children by providing them with unlimited pleasures. Ireneus was the first great Christian to think this way.[3.]

This perspective of life is, of course, exquisitely spelt out in Bunyan's *Pilgrim's Progress.* Without the exposure to Evil or Sin, and the opportunity to make faulty choices, how could the virtues of, for instance, courage, unselfishness or compassion develop? Ireneus' philosophy and Bunyan's famous allegory both invoke a return to the question posed earlier: How can a powerful God really be Love, when tragedy, wickedness and suffering exist so extensively around us?

The Christian Explanation.

Any answer to such a question can only be in terms of faith - not fact. If one can abandon the medieval concept of a God with a long beard sitting on a throne in heaven, and one can think instead of God as being simply "Existence" in itself, or "Reality", then we can choose to infer "His" nature according to our different understandings of the world around us as each one individually perceives it. Such a philosophy allows everyone complete freedom of choice, and Christians collectively are free to accept a concept of God that they will gladly admit derives from their own understanding of Jesus Christ. It then becomes entirely reasonable to accept the tenet of St John: "Love is of God for God is Love."

To accomplish such a mental and spiritual leap can only be expressed as an act of faith, but that way seems to a great many people to make more sense of life than not to make such a leap. In any case, those who prefer not to are entirely at liberty in their choice!

As Teilhard de Chardin has written in *Le Milieu Divin*: "The work which God has undertaken in uniting himself intimately to the created beings, presupposes in them a slow preparation in the course of which they cannot avoid the risks involved in the imperfect ordering of the world around them; and on the other hand, because the final victory of Good over Evil can only be completed in the total organisation of the world, our infinitely short lives could not possibly hope to know the joy of entry into the Promised Land."[4]

References.

1. Plato, *The Republic* (Macmillan), 1921, ii, p.379
2. Hick, J. *Evil and the God of Love* (Collins), 1966, p.217 ff
3. Op. cit. p.283
4. Teilhard de Chardin, *Le Milieu Divin* (Fontana), 1957, p.85

Suffering

I find that I can think about *evil* as an impersonal influence that confronts all mankind all the time, but by contrast I can only understand *suffering* as a very personal individual distress. I don't think this is professional bias, because many forms of suffering are misfortunes that may afflict any one of us at any time, and are not necessarily illnesses.

I accept that my definition of *'sin'* is theologically simplistic because I am content to define it as the deliberate choice of an action that is clearly perceived to be not the best moral choice, regardless of all other considerations.

The terms Evil, Suffering and Sin are only words, but words are needed to convey thought. As I understand *'religion'*, it is a realm of ideas and thoughts fraught with possibilities for misunderstanding (which may explain why theologians tend to use so many words to explain these ideas.)

In the Bible different persons use these different words at different times. Their different meanings must be briefly examined because people are often confused by them.

The ancient prophets of the Old Testament preached time and time again that God would punish man for his evil ways and that mankind would suffer for the consequences of those sins. They taught that their God was good and almighty, but also that He was a Just and Fair God who punished wrong-doing by the infliction of suffering; God's punishment for sin was suffering.

In early Judaism, Evil was thought of as a Power in opposition to God (rather than an immoral act), therefore God's people must not become enslaved to this opposing Power. This idea, which originated in the animistic religions, was still the norm for the ancient Jews.

An important religious insight follows from this Old Testament concept as it is expressed most clearly in the Ten Commandments (Ex. Ch. 20), *viz:* that a civilised society cannot thrive and prosper if it persistently flouts the rules by which it is sustained. If it continues to do so, then such a society will collapse.

Later however, about the 5th century BC the unknown writer of the story of Job perceived that suffering, wretchedness and misery are *not* only the experience of sinners and evil-doers, and his marvellous story challenges the older view of the Prophets because he realised that many blind, crippled, hungry and starving people have led blameless lives while, on the contrary, many prosperous, well-fed and healthy people were sometimes undoubted sinners! One can be fairly confident that the marvellous ancient writer of the Book of Job would be able to make similar observations about British (and other) society today; nevertheless it was a profound new religious perception when spelt out in the story of Job, 500 years before Christ.

Jesus taught differently again, and this seems to me to be far more important. You have only to read any gospel to see that Jesus went about healing all sorts of people who experienced all sorts of distress. It must follow logically, therefore, that if Jesus was God, or the Son of God, he just *could not* go around healing people *if* their suffering was specifically imposed on them by the will of God.

I find it not only amazing, but also very sad, that so many Christian people do believe, even today, that suffering is God's inflicted punishment for sin. But I have met this many times among my patients and friends: "Why has God done this to me?" they ask. No Christian should feel like that, because the whole life and ministry of Jesus Christ completely refutes such an idea. That very primitive concept of regarding suffering as being inflicted by God as a specific punishment is totally rebutted by the Gospel accounts of Jesus' Healing Ministry. That is why the Healing Ministry is such an important part of the Christian Gospel. (c.f. p. 171-172)

Jesus' Suffering.

It has been declared earlier that the crucifixion may not have been due to the treachery of Judas, the incompetence of Pilate or even as an atoning sacrifice.

Placation of the Gods by sacrifice was certainly associated with primitive animistic religious ritual, but as declared earlier, Jesus' cruel death demonstrated, and demonstrated perfectly clearly, that His revelations about God, and that His beliefs about God, are true, and that He was so certain of this that he was prepared to die for it, in spite of the hostility, the mockery, and the disbelief of worldly people regarding His Teaching and Ministry.

Despite the ingenuity of wicked men today, is any more dreadful suffering imaginable? I find it simply misleading to use the words 'sacrifice' or 'ransom', or 'redemption' to describe Jesus' terrible ordeal.

But the crucifixion does tell us a tremendous truth about suffering, *viz:* if Jesus was in conflict with worldly thinking, then we who seek to follow Him must also be prepared to meet with hostility and disbelief. "He taught that anyone who would follow Him in living by the Truth must always carry on his back the stake for his own execution."[1.]

Suffering Today.

Everyone can understand the implication of the suffering that goes with illness, accident or bereavement - but that is only a small part of the subject. The consequences that arise from misfortunes such as chronic disability, unemployment or prolonged poverty are likewise only another small part of the total suffering that mankind endures.

Nobody can make the journey through life without meeting and striving to come to terms with the anguish and distress of suffering. It seems to be an inescapable component of our human condition.

Consider business life and the suffering that may be experienced by the man of integrity (someone like Job). For instance, the businessman whose partner embezzles; or the clerk whose office manager gives him dishonest instructions (I have known two different men who, when put into this predicament, immediately resigned their livelihoods); or the man in the workshop whose mate never pulls his weight (but is not found out); and so on.

The man of integrity may suffer extremely unless his conscience becomes dulled by the continuous stress of the situation.

Then what about the suffering we all inflict on the social "outsider" by our thoughtlessness? If he has a skin as dark, say, as that of Jesus, he may find England a tough place. There may be no room for him at the inn. Or what of the visitor to our church if nobody speaks to him? (One particular visitor was shown to a pew, but kept his hat on; so the sidesman politely explained that he should remove it, but the visitor declined. The sidesman consulted the vicar, who was perplexed and came himself to enquire: "Is there a particular reason?" he asked. "Yes," was the reply, "I've been coming to this church for three months but this is the first time anyone has spoken to me.").

Patients with psychological illnesses or AIDS *more often than not* suffer from ostracism. Fifty years ago it was tuberculosis or syphilis, or niggers and wogs; before that there was plague and leprosy, but we still look askance at germs, or skin pigment, or strangers.

Then how much suffering do we all cause one another by thoughtless remarks and gossip? Far more than we would like to admit to. Trivial innuendos can be hurtful and the cumulative effect of this is to cloud our awareness of delicate human feelings and to blind ourselves to the manifestations of God in our fellow men and women. Is the ninth of the Ten Commandments obsolete: "Thou shalt not bear false witness against thy neighbour" (Ex. Ch. 20, 16)?

For a last example, what about the suffering of

loneliness? What about the isolation of Jesus in Gethsemane? Those who have literally nobody to confide in are the lonely ones, and yet they are often our *neighbours*.

All these people, lonely or hurt by the things we say, social outsiders or distressed at work; these people are all around us and they provide you and me with the opportunity to create from their distress the richer experience of compassion and joy.

It seems to me to be in the nature of things generally that experience, or "God", always builds on what already exists; compassion and caring can only develop against a background of suffering or distress. I believe it is important to realise this. If we are to "Love our neighbours", that is, to exercise real compassion toward them, we have to cultivate a sensitive awareness of suffering; if we do not, we are likely to shut out the awareness of Love as well. You cannot be a Christian without contemplating the crucifixion. The quality of our Christianity must be measured by our concern for others which is why the Christian must put Love and Compassion at the heart of things.

Reference.

1. Baker, J.A. *The Foolishness of God* (Darton Longman and Todd) 1970, p.403

Fear

It is important that any consideration of Love, Evil and Suffering should also include Fear, because fear has much more to do with these matters than we usually realise.

It was noticed earlier that *homo sapiens* was almost certainly living on this wonderful world for at least 50,000 years before we arrived to 'take it over' from our forebears. How did they succeed in surviving in those early times? Well, no matter how politely we may try to dress it up, they managed to survive largely by sheer cunning; which is only another way of saying that they combined fear, terror, alarm and dismay with intelligence, reason, skill, and a good deal of luck!

If our own direct ancestors had not succeeded for about two thousand generations in dodging the perils of the jungle which beset them during those many thousands of years in caves, hunting and fighting for food, then obviously not one of us could be alive today. We have no record of those ancient ancestors of ours until, as has been suggested, 'the curtain went up' about ten thousand years ago.

Fear is more basic to survival than almost any other of our faculties, and we cannot ignore its involvement with religion. Primitive man undoubtedly lived for many millennia a life that was substantially directed by it. Whether expressed physically or mentally, fear is a very powerful force in life. It has to be, because without fear, and the capacity to respond to it intelligently, primitive mankind could not possibly have survived the assaults of the jungle. This primitive existence, based on fear and the competition to survive, lasted for many generations. Without a sufficient and lively *fear,* one can confidently assert that one or other of our ancestors would have succumbed, and each one of us depends on every single ancestor to bring us into existence. You cannot omit the odd ancestor whom you may not like!

Some time after "the curtain went up," and as those ancestors were becoming *homo religiosus,* we find some of our earliest clues about them at the beginning of the Old Testament. In the Genesis legend, almost the very first encounter of man with God states that "Adam hid, *because he was afraid"!* (Gen. Ch. 3,10)

If you examine the Old Testament to discover what it has to say about fear you will find, time and time again, and in all sorts of places, that the writers of the Old Testament are nearly always struggling against fear! The Book about Jonah is one of the really great stories about Fear.

This attribute *"fear,"* which so helped our ancient ancestors to survive, is opposed over and over again in the Old Testament, which keeps declaring in one form or another: "Fear not ..."

"I sought the Lord and he heard me and delivered me from all my fears" (Ps. 34,4). "They cried to the Lord in their troubles and he saved them out of their distresses" (Ps. 107, 13. "I will trust and not be afraid" (Is. Ch. 12, 2). "Be strong and of good courage, dread not, nor be dismayed." (I Chr, Ch. 22, 13).

There are many such declarations in the Old Testament, but it is reasonable to say that they are adequately summarised in Ecclesiastes: "Fear God and keep his commandments, for this is the whole duty of Man." (Ecc. Ch. 12, 13).

Fear in broad general terms becomes narrowed down to *"fear God"*. It does seem, therefore, that all this points to a very important conclusion, *viz.* that Mankind has progressively evolved through the ages, using his mind, his intelligence and his reason, all the time learning how better to come to terms with fear. This suggests that a primitive fear helped him to survive all those millennia of immaturity, "rehearsing" (as described earlier) for mankind's advance toward a more and more wonderful, deeper, richer, concept of God and this marvellous world. In more recent centuries it does seem possible that mankind may be becoming less dependent on that basic protective fear, and that, rather like a child learning to swim, he may be very gradually discovering that he can depend more and more on his own God-given intelligence, skill and reason. Can it perhaps be that this is what God is gently teaching us, generation by generation?

Certainly man's religion as it is told in the Bible is a story of progressive change. The Adam legend has already been referred to; if you examine the history of the Jewish people as recounted in the Bible, for instance in II Kings Ch. 17, you find a description of that earlier animistic religion that gave way before the Old Testament Prophets and the Judaic Law. Later, Job's teaching about suffering marks another remarkable advance in mankind's religious thought.

Jesus preached and taught yet a further forward step, and a very big step indeed. The uncomfortable dilemma about Jesus was (and still is) that He did not keep to the Jewish rules, but nevertheless taught about God with a devastating confidence. Whoever could such a Person as this be? This disturbing question frightened some people. He simply declared that a person-to-person relationship of respect and compassion is what matters most in life's affairs, and that to live by such principles is better than meticulous deference to the Judaic Law (Matt. Chs 5 - 7). Such teaching obviously threatened many peoples' livelihoods. It jeopardised the whole structure of the society they depended on. Similar situations have occurred over and over again in recent secular history. The people of His day (and since) could not commit themselves to His radical ideas about human relationships; so *because they were afraid* and felt themselves threatened, they killed Him.

Can we today do without fear? Of course not! It is just as necessary for our protection today as it was for our primitive ancestors - but in a more sophisticated and complicated way. Unfortunately there is a real risk that sometimes fear can get out of control, and then it can ruin a person. It is the commonest complication of any illness; every good doctor must learn that, and be able to recognise and diagnose it. Fear can also lead us to make wrong decisions, and simply because of fear we may wrongly choose to sin. Every priest or minister needs to understand that. Fear can and does provoke greed, injustice, crime, terrorism or murder. Everyone in society who is in some way responsible for reaching a judgement about his neighbour (eg patient, client, employee, friend or enemy) needs to be quite clear about that. Fear can lead communities or nations into war with each other.

I do profoundly believe that Jesus has given us the guidance and teaching that we all need to keep our fears in their proper place. It is all in the Sermon on the Mount. He spells out the way that modern, more mature mankind can live together. To demonstrate this by example cost Him His life at the hands of our forefathers. Christianity is not easy, because *each one of us has to make choices.* Jesus invites us to prefer the way of Love rather than the way of Greed or Power.

St Paul put it succinctly to the Ephesians (Ch. 5, 2): "Walk in Love as Christ has also loved us." St John put it even more briefly (I John, Ch. 4, 18): "Perfect Love casteth out fear."

The Christian life declares that in trying to live this way, the Way of Love, we shall be better able to find the strength to wrestle with our fears, to bear our suffering, and to resist evil.

The Christian Emphasis Changes Through the Centuries

(The Early Church.The Incarnation. The Medieval Church. The Reformation. John Wesley.)

To understand the significance of Christianity in the world today, it is necessary to understand something of how and why it has altered since the time of Christ. Although the Church has made many mistakes - usually more obvious in retrospect than at the time - the influence of Jesus Christ continues to be extraordinarily vibrant and apposite today. I make no apology that in this next section, an Englishman is thinking primarily about Christianity in England. It is fair comment to say that many important external influences are omitted; and that the whole section may be biased!

I do try to demonstrate that neither Christian Belief nor Christian Behaviour are rigid and static, but that, marvellously, century by century in a changing world, Christianity continues to "change its clothes" to meet the needs of succeeding generations of men and women who seek to understand the real Gospel of Jesus.

Advances in scholarship during the past hundred years or so have probably enabled us to know more about the Early Church than in any previous century since Constantine. We must be grateful for this, and accept it. My own belief about the Incarnation is more sympathetic to Nestorius of Constantinople than to Apollinaris of Laodicea - (see page 110) for which heresy some of my friends may think I should be burned at the stake!

Fortunately for me, the Church has become a little wiser and considerably more tolerant since the Renaissance.

I think it is astonishing how Christianity survived so much superstition during the Middle Ages - E.W. Barnes' simile of the buds on a tree in springtime seems marvellously apt (see page 41). I cannot do justice to the many different influences that arose from the Reformation, but I do believe that in England the Wesleyan Revival should be perceived as the logical culmination of the changes which the Reformation brought about, thus enabling England to adapt to a rapidly changing social structure arising from the industrial revolution.

The Early Church

Reliable information is scarce about the very earliest developments of The Christian Church; but for anyone to understand the situation today, even just in England, it is useful to examine what is known of how the church has developed. In many ways it is like a tree, gradually becoming taller, with some smaller and some bigger branches; sometimes having to be pruned, but growing to shelter a wider and wider area, with its roots extending out of sight in unknown directions.

The Apostolic Period.

There is no single pattern of Ministry in the New Testament. The Epistles dictated by St Paul only reflect human affairs in those Churches where he was influential. The 'Acts of the Apostles' is a continuation of St Luke's Gospel. The authenticity of the remaining Epistles is still uncertain.

However, any small gathering of people needs some sort of management and organisation. This applies to all movements in human affairs as they expand from their very beginnings. The Earliest Church in any one place at first comprised little more than a few households; but obviously its meetings, their venues, and its business would have to be arranged. Someone had to be responsible for doing this, and this pattern is widely reflected in the New Testament. One can discern broadly similar patterns unfolding in the growth of, for instance, the National Trust or the Royal Society, or in the progressive development of representative democracy in the parliaments of the world. What begins as a compelling idea or a movement of the human spirit, as it is received and accepted and starts to grow, must of necessity become organised. It begins to need structure, and like the skeleton in relation to flesh and blood it gradually becomes rigid in its form and therefore more difficult to alter later on.

At the same time language differences can be a problem. There were almost certainly linguistic difficulties between the Aramaic and Greek speaking Christians in Jerusalem, which led to seven of the Greek speaking community being selected to look after their fellow Christians. They were called deacons (Acts Ch. 6, 3). But there is no precise information in the New Testament as to their work. By the time of I Timothy (Ch. 3), the qualities appropriate to a deacon differed little from those of a bishop.

As the Apostles and Prophets died, and as the longing for an imminent "Second coming of Christ" inevitably receded, the Christian communities which they had founded moved into a new era, in which no one remained alive who had actually known Jesus; but the little communities certainly went on increasing in number and spreading geographically at an extraordinary rate.

The Post-Apostolic Period.

In the pastoral Epistles, now thought to have been written in the second century rather than by St Paul, the role of the Leader of these Christian communities is more clearly expressed and two grades have appeared, bishops and deacons. Presbyters, or elders, are mentioned, nearly always in the plural, as if they may have comprised an inner circle of responsible people to help with the arrangements of the Church community and its caring for the flock. There was no "Christian Tradition" to refer to in those days!

Beside the "management responsibilities", there appear to have been other individuals with different charismatic gifts. These are mentioned in Romans (Ch. 12, 4 - 8), I Cor (Ch. 12), and Eph. (Ch. 4, 11 - 16) but it is difficult today to know just what their functions were in those times. The early Church certainly needed some sort of organisation, but it also contained people with Gifts of the Spirit, or Charisma, that did not quite fit into a systematic structure: eg such gifts as teaching, healing, caring for the poor, the sick, the bereaved, and the dying.

As the Church grew and spread, various individuals such as these, who were considered to be possessed of more distinct holiness, either founded or joined special Religious Orders, or became acknowledged as "Saints" because of the special Christian quality seen in their lives. This was the way that the Church acknowledged the 'overflow' of spirituality while at the same time preserving its institutional structure.

So by about the third century, the Church seems to have been held together collectively by Bishops as Leaders with the most senior responsibility for each community, and these *to some extent* conferring, supporting, or disagreeing with each other. In their various localities they were assisted by Presbyters (Elders), and Deacons. Such leaders seem to have emerged or come forward by the acclamation of their own separate communities. St Augustine of Hippo appears to have been thus "called" against his own inclination:

"The aged Bishop, Valerius, addressed his flock assembled in the Church, urging them to find a candidate for the priesthood *; they laid hands on Augustine and brought him forward; the Bishop therefore ordained him priest in the tumultuous fashion of that age."[1.] (AD 391)

Any regional unity of belief or conduct at this time depended on the neighbouring leaders meeting together. What little literature is available from this early period suggests a wide variety of belief and organisation, and some disagreements, but the Church was nevertheless held together by the Charisma of the Risen Christ!

There is no satisfactory evidence from history which supports the doctrine of the so-called "Apostolic Succession" by the laying on of hands as being valid from Apostolic times; all the evidence points to the various leaders being chosen by the corporate communities which, knowing them, decided to invoke their leadership. Thus we realise that a great deal of Church doctrine originated not from Jesus Christ but from the centuries that followed.

References.

1. *Encyclopaedia Britannica* (14th Ed.)
2. For some of these ideas I am indebted to the teaching of the Rt. Revd. John Austin Baker at various times.

(*'Priesthood' will be considered later in relation to the medieaval church. See pages 119-120)

The Incarnation

The Doctrine of the Incarnation is less important to Christianity than that of the Resurrection. Although from very early times the Young Church pondered deeply about the "nature" of Jesus Christ, it was not until the Council of Chalcedon in 451 AD that a "formula" stating an official doctrine of the Church was declared. Today the language of that 'Declaration of Chalcedon' seems lengthy and cumbersome. Collins Dictionary is more succinct. It defines the Christian Incarnation as: "The taking on of human form and nature, by Jesus as the Son of God." For present purposes this is good enough.

To a modern intelligent person such a definition of the Incarnation Doctrine understandably raises a variety of questions that nowadays simply cannot be brushed aside. The question "Who was Jesus?" is a question that demands an answer.

Curiosity comes naturally to most people. Devising hypothetical explanations for the various natural phenomena that we perceive also seems to come naturally to many of us. It is the way we are made; many of us would happily say that such reflective curiosity is part of God's wonderful gift in our creation. But at all stages of mankind's development, the answers we devise to explain anything at all are determined by the knowledge and understanding available to us at that particular time. Different terminology is inevitably preferred to explain the same phenomena to people of different cultures in different periods of history.

For instance, the early Greeks believed that all material things derived from Earth, Fire, Air or Water. But that is not good enough for a modern physicist. Likewise, Hippocratic medicine taught that bodily disorders could be diagnosed in terms of the four humours: blood, phlegm, yellow bile and black bile. The twentieth century knowledge of body chemistry has made such hypotheses untenable.

So, among the early Christians, convinced of the Resurrection of Jesus Christ, the question was bound to arise: *who can this Jesus really be, whom we know did live, was executed, and rose again?*

We have always to remember that the earliest Christians were Jews. Inevitably their pondering about the nature of Jesus was strongly influenced by their Jewish contemporary thought and ideas. Jesus himself proclaimed God as "Father", so it is not unreasonable to find him sometimes referred to as the "Son". Also, the term "Son of God" (Ps. 2, 7) was used in Judaism as part of the coronation ritual for their ancient kings, expressing the idea of divine adoption on attaining kingship. The same idea occurred widely, too, in primitive society.[1.]

St Paul, a trained Pharisee, attributed such divine status to Jesus from the time of the Resurrection: (Acts Ch. 13, 32-37); St Mark ascribes divine Sonhood to the moment of baptism (Mk, Ch. 1, 10-11); St Luke takes the divine Sonhood back to Christ's birth (Lk. Ch. 1, 35), meaning that Jesus had no Father apart from God. Probably in that Apostolic period Jesus, like the kings of Judah, was simply being acclaimed as appointed by God to exercise his rule over the world.[2,3,4.]

Early Christianity was exposed to Hellenistic ways of thought as well as Jewish, and in those earliest Churches some sort of belief that Jesus was divine was an acceptable idea to people of either Hellenistic or Jewish origin. So we find that St Paul can write in Rom. Ch. 8, 3: "God...by sending his son in a form like our own"; or "God sent His own Son" (Gal. Ch. 4, 4). It is important to notice that although such phrases may be thought to imply pre-existence, they do not identify the Son with the Father. It remains unclear whether that Early Church thought of Jesus as having any pre-existence before "He came down from Heaven".

Thus some sort of Incarnational Doctrine began to emerge very early in the history of the Church, but this then led to further intellectual difficulties. If Jesus was the "Son of God" *in reality* rather than by title, then *how exactly* did He become a fully human man? Why, if He was really divine, should He adopt human form at all? *How could* He be both wholly human *and* wholly divine at the same time? Was the purpose of His becoming human perhaps in some way to make atonement for human sin, possibly similar to Abraham's offer to sacrifice Isaac (Gen. Ch. 22)? Or, was Jesus with His own human life 'ransoming' mankind from servitude to Evil? St Paul certainly thought this way (cf Rom. Ch. 3, 24; Rom.. Ch. 5, 8; Rom. Ch. 8, 3) and the Early Church understood. (It must be remembered that in the normal thought of that period it was believed that everyone was under some kind of ownership - our modern concept of "freedom" was unknown. If mankind was owned by the Evil Power, then surely God could redeem mankind by paying the appropriate ransom?)

Other intellectual difficulties similar to these inevitably made the earliest concept of the Christian Incarnation more complicated. Unfortunately, as the Early Church extended during the second and third centuries AD, its leaders became increasingly convinced that it was necessary to find answers in respect of such questions regarding the origin of Jesus. If they had been content to designate Jesus as the "Son of God" and to admit boldly that such an ancient title was not definable in human terms, then Christian theology might have been spared much bitter controversy, and the real challenge and impact of Jesus' Ministry and Gospel for human living and conduct might have been more obvious to the world.

A. Nolan [5.] offers this interpretation of the divinity of Jesus: he asserts that every person has a "God" (certainly genuine atheists are rare!), and by "God" Nolan implies something which gives real meaning to existence for that person, eg money, power, prestige, love, career, etc. He asserts that to believe that Jesus is "divine" is another way of stating that Christians accept Him and what He stands for as "God" - their top-priority in life. Christians therefore deduce their idea of "God" from what we *do know* about Jesus. In other words, we argue from Jesus toward God, not from what we think we know about God toward understanding Jesus. To say that Jesus is divine does not change our understanding of Jesus but it does change our understanding of 'divinity'. It turns our understanding away from money, power, prestige, etc. and the 'old' former ideas about God, to find our God in Jesus and the things He stood for. Nolan suggests that

Jesus claimed to understand "Truth", that He was utterly absorbed by "Truth", and that in Him the "Truth became flesh".

Marcion, and also Gnostic Heresies.

As the debate about who Jesus could be unfolded during the second and third centuries, some of the proffered explanations and objections must be noticed. They are important for the understanding of the Incarnation Doctrine.

. One of the earliest figures in the debate was Marcion, [6.] the son of the Bishop of Sinope, who came to Rome from Pontus is Asia Minor about 120 AD, hoping to take an active part in propagating the Christian Faith. He was a follower of St Paul with an intellectual approach to St Paul's philosophy of "Love". Marcion had concluded that according to St Paul (there was no New Testament then!) the God who was the Father of Jesus Christ was a God of Mercy, whereas the God of the Jews in the Old Testament seemed to him to be a vindictive and jealous God, but who nevertheless stood for justice and law (dualism?). Thus he earned the hostility of Jewish Christians, by preferring the God of St Paul, viz "Love", being well aware that St Paul's teaching predated some of the other documents then in circulation. He quarrelled with the Leaders of Roman Christianity, and in 144 AD he left Rome, and his writings were destroyed.

Gnosticism was (and still is) difficult to describe concisely. It was as much a religious attitude as a belief, and it existed in a variety of forms. Its most important feature was probably its dualistic concept of a world of good and evil. It was particularly prevalent in the second and third centuries AD and probably derived much of its philosophy from Greek thought. It certainly had features in common with Mithraism. It offered an explanation of the Christian Incarnation by positing that Jesus was really a divine God and only "appeared" to be human. Those Christians who accepted this gnostic heresy were known as Docetists and their polytheistic views of a divine Jesus also tended in the second century to separate Christian thought from the Judaic emphasis on monotheism. The extreme gnostic influences on Christianity not only denied that Jesus had ever been truly a man, but even alleged that he only 'seemed' to suffer crucifixion!

Arius and Constantine.

During the second and third centuries AD a number of different views about the nature of the Christ-figure developed, but at the beginning of the fourth century, *acceptance* of Christianity by the Emperor Constantine, introduced an important new influence to the scene. Constantine, as a statesman, shrewdly perceived that while Christianity was gaining support throughout his empire (mainly vis-a-vis Mithraism), there was dissension among its leaders which he determined to eliminate so that this "new religion" could be assimilated more harmoniously by his people to become the new state religion of the Roman Empire.

The most important heresy at this time was Arianism. Arius was troubled by the thought that if Jesus Christ was

God, and the "Father" of Jesus Christ was also God, then there must be two Gods, and so Christianity had to be a form of polytheism. He therefore allowed Christ every conceivable honour short of Godhead: a 'special creation', a 'son of God', a demi-God - but no more than that. God remained supreme. Such a separation between God (the "Father" or Supreme Creator), and Christ (the 'Son' or demi-God), certainly preserved Judaic monotheism, but it seemed to allow the Supreme Creator to drift away as a cold abstraction. However the orthodox position, by asserting that Christ is God, also implies that God is Christlike; thus the Supreme Creator is, in the human sense, not unknowable, but is also *good*. The logical consequence of *that* conviction also seemed to be that if the Son suffered (crucifixion), then the Father suffered crucifixion too. Many people were uneasy about accepting this; the Greek concept of the immutability of God was very real to them.

The opposing concepts of Jewish monotheism and Greek gnosticism thus clash in Arianism. Broadly speaking, the Western part of the Roman Empire accepted the orthodox Christian belief; but Arianism prevailed as a strong dissenting influence in the Eastern part.

Constantine intervened because he was determined to eliminate such dissension so that he could declare a unanimous belief as the new state religion. He convened the Council of Nicea in 325 AD and presided over it himself. Most of the 275 Bishops who attended were Eastern. Eusebius of Caesarea represented the Arian standpoint and Constantine called upon him publicly to accept the insertion of the phrase *"of one substance with the Father."*

into the credal statement that Euslebius was himself proposing. He weakly gave way. [7]

The outcome was that the creed formulated at Nicea led to the development of one party led by Apollinaris, Bishop of Laodicea, which emphasised the divinity of Christ, and another led by Nestorius, Bishop of Constantinople, emphasising his manhood. Thus the controversy was inflamed into a major issue which persisted until the Council of Chalcedon in 451 AD.

The Virgin Birth.

In the development of the Incarnational Doctrine, the question was bound to arise as to how, if Jesus was divine, did He become a fully human Man? The birth stories in the Gospels of St Matthew (Matt. Ch. 1, 18 - 25) and St Luke (Lk. Ch. 2, 11 - 19) were written not earlier than 80 AD and are suspected of being even later insertions. The Virgin Birth idea was apparently unknown to St Paul! So just how and when did the story of the Virgin Birth originate? It does not matter! By the fourth century it had become an established part of the Incarnation Doctrine.

Today the doctrine of the Virgin Birth is historically dubious, and physiologically untenable. G. Vermes [8] argues an irrefutable case for acknowledging the story as myth. This explanation of the origin of Jesus which traces his status as "Son of God" back even earlier than Resurrection, Baptism or Birth (ie to Conception) originated nearly two thousand years ago and was based on physiological concepts now well known to be inaccurate. In those days it was believed that, like a seed germinating in the soil, the paternal sperm planted within the maternal uterus became the embryo. Chromosomes, genes and zygotes were undreamed of! It would now be honest to abandon the belief entirely.

Habgood [9.] has pointed out that the Virgin Birth story was a 'safeguard' against Docetism - to draw attention to the genuine humanity of Jesus (but does it?), and he also considers that the Virgin Birth story emphasises the universal significance of Jesus Christ, and that the story still has value as myth.

The Chalcedonian Declaration.

The question for theologians today is whether the explanation reached at Chalcedon after four centuries of uncertainty still remains adequate for modern thought. Gore [10.] Baker [11.] and Hick [12.] (many references), all express important views on this matter.

C. Butler [13.] reminds us that the Declaration of Chalcedon, for all its shortcomings, was probably the best expression *in words* of the Christian Truth, *as it was understood in those times*. He observes that the Christian Gospel is not merely an intellectual accomplishment but that it reveals *LOVE,* teaching that God is to be identified with our destination and fate.

John A. T. Robinson believed that the supernatural view of the Incarnation could never rid itself of the idea of the "prince who appears in the guise of a beggar" [14.] and that for this reason too, it can perfectly well be acknowledged as myth; but he also believed that the story should survive to indicate the profound significance of the events.

It took the Church a very long time indeed to evolve the Chalcedonian declaration, but is that a good reason why it should remain inviolable more than one thousand years later? Christopher Bryant [15.] one of the Cowley Fathers, has written: "Christianity burst upon the world in the first century as a message about God and His purpose for Man. It was expressed inevitably in the language and ideas current in that day. Many of the assumptions, for instance about cosmology, the all persuasive influence of demons, and the shortly to be expected end of the world, seem to us to be mistaken or irrelevant. If the gospel is to make on people of the 20th century anything like the impact it made on men of the first century, it will have to be interwoven with beliefs and ideas that are important today. The cutting edge, as well as the liberating power of the gospel can only be preserved if it comes to terms with the discoveries of Modern Science and the new knowledge which has transformed the outlook of men and women today. CHRISTIANITY WAS AN EXPERIENCE BEFORE IT WAS A THEOLOGY." [15.]

Today, very many thoughtful people accept the teaching, example and gospel of Jesus Christ, and manifest the Love of God in their own lives; but sometimes they find the supernatural Incarnation Doctrine a stumbling block. They confess "Jesus is Lord", but dissociate themselves from the organised Christian denominations of the Church, often for the reasons mentioned above.

Many people find so much myth in relation to the Incarnation that it often appears to a modern educated person to be more aligned with primitive superstition rather than with the triumphant Pauline declaration (Rom. Ch. 8, 39):

"Nothing in all Creation can separate us from the Love of God which is in Christ Jesus Our Lord."

References.

1. Fraser, J.G. *The Golden Bough* (Macmillan & Co), 1922, abb. edition, 1941.
2. Pannenberg *The Apostles Creed in the Light of Today's Questions* 1972, p.61f
3. Burnaby, J. *The Belief of Christendom* (S.P.C.K.) 1959, pp 65-67
4. Vermes, G. *Jesus the Jew* 1973, p86-212
5. Nolan, A. *Jesus before Christianity* (Darton, Longmann, Todd) 1977, p136ff
6. Somervell, D.C. *A Short History of our Religion* (Bell & Sons Lond), 1922, p.114
7. Jones, A.H.M. *The Decline of the Ancient World* (Longmans) 1966, p.43
8. Vermes, G. ibid p.213
9. Habgood, J. *Confessions of a Conservative Liberal* (S.P.C.K.) 1988, p.60
10. Gore, C. *Lux Mundi* (1899), p.159
11. Baker, J. A. *The Foolishness of God* (Darton, Longman and Todd) 1970, p.242
12. Hick, J. *The Myth of God Incarnate* (S.C.M. Press) 1947
13. Butler, C. *The Truth of God Incarnate* (Hodder & Stoughton) 1977, p.99
14. Robinson, J.A.T. *Honest to God* (S.C.M.) 1963, p.65ff
15. Bryant, C. *The River Within* pp. 4-5

The Mediaeval Church

No attempt to understand the Christian Church to-day can be adequate without recognising how enormously it altered in nature and organisation during the thousand years or so between the time of Constantine the Great (Roman Emperor, 306-337), and the Reformation.

Constantine.

Constantine, as already mentioned, determined to nationalise the Christian Church, thereby acknowledging that Christianity had grown steadily in its influence and support in many parts of the Empire. By the fourth century AD the ancient Mediterranean world had virtually lost its primitive polytheistic faiths, and neither Greek philosophy nor stoicism, the oriental mystery religions, nor even the Jewish religion, was at that time offering much to support the declining Roman civilisation. The Christian Church had advantages that attracted the statesmanship of Constantine. It was bound by no local or racial ties, it was universal; even if it did not always live up to its ideals, at least it declared them and proclaimed a lofty rule of conduct. It offered women respect and chivalry, and slaves equality before God with the freeman. To a considerable extent it owed its rapid spread across the Empire to its influence over women and slaves in the households of the Empire.

After Constantine had issued the "Edict of Milan" in 313: "... concerning the Christians, all who choose that religion are to be permitted to continue therein without let or hindrance and are not to be in any way troubled or molested ..." Christianity quickly responded to this invitation and soon became the accepted religion of the Empire. It became more numerous. It became a wealthy, powerful and well organised institution, but sadly, in contrast to the tolerant paganism which it superseded, it became exclusive and intolerant toward other beliefs. A hundred years after Constantine, (under the Emperor Theodosius, who established the Nicene Creed as the official religious belief of the Roman Empire), Christians were persecuting pagans.

Whether the Roman Empire really took over Christianity, or whether it would be truer to consider that Christianity took over the Empire is unclear, but Constantine certainly considered himself to be Head of the Church by presiding in person over the Council of Nicea in 325 AD. His assumption of such precedence does not seem to have been opposed by the bishops of the day, and thus the immemorial relationship of the sacerdotal office of the priest and the secular responsibility of the king was gradually resumed as the Christian Church became the official religion of the Empire and eliminated its rivals.

In four centuries the Church had changed Christianity drastically from the straightforward teaching about Love which Jesus had imparted by the Sea of Galilee, to become an instrument of the state. The Nicene Creed is a poor substitute for the Sermon on the Mount, and all branches of "The Church" were diminished in stature and leadership as a result.

Nevertheless the Church steadily refused to baptise

any gladiator unless he pledged himself to abandon that vocation, and the last gladiatorial show in the Western Empire was in 404 AD. The slave and the slave-owner knelt together at Communion, and the ceremony of freeing slaves (manumission) was placed under the control of the clergy. But it was not until the thirteenth century that slavery might be said to have almost disappeared from Europe, passing insensibly into serfdom.

As men began to concentrate on saving their own souls, forgetting the Gospel of Love preached by Jesus, certain primitive religious practices crept into the life of the Church. Various forms of abstinence thus came to be seen as Christian virtues. Hermits renounced society; fasting enhanced the numinous; restraint from sexual intercourse allowed the holy person to express the priority of devotion to God. Abstinence is found in the animistic religions and Islam, as well as Christianity. But these practices enabled the medieval Church to develop the celibate priesthood (even if concubinage was widespread), and strengthened the monastic orders. Through these it had substantial (particularly economic) advantage in staffing hospitals to care for the sick and dying, monasteries to promote study and knowledge, shelter for travellers (which made journeys safer), and convents to save (in many instances) the spinster or widow from begging or prostitution. Later, different aspects of abstinence developed: Puritanism in England, Calvinism in Geneva, and the Exercises of the Jesuits.

For the early Christians, the boundary between the spirit of Christ and the spirit of the world lay in their baptism. But with the massive expansion of the Church after the Edict of Milan (although not all its formal adherents were baptised), this boundary gradually changed to become a distinction between the more exalted 'office-bearers' in the church (ie the clergy) and the more lowly 'believers' (ie the laity). Thus two classes of Christian people were differentiated. Clericalisation had begun!

This two-tier Christianity is still cherished by a substantial proportion of clergy, and accepted by a significant proportion of laity.

The Feudal System.

While the Church was still adjusting to the changes instigated by Constantine, and the decline of Roman secular power, it had also to adjust to the developing feudal system and its implications for European Society.

In the course of these changes, the powerful nobles swore fealty to the emperor, now claiming to be head of the Church as well as the state, so it followed that their "Christianisation" similarly involved the allegiance of their vassals. Society did not then cater for individuals to voice their own private consciences, but rather bade them to accept without question the decisions of their overlord. It was therefore not unreasonable that sometimes these nobles built "private churches", both to enhance their status on earth, and also to help ensure a smoother path toward heaven after death. In the course of these changes, the bishops of the Church managed to retain their spiritual autonomy, but the kings and dukes held on to the secular power. This meant that the *ecclesia* shifted from being a living Christian community to becoming a status symbol for the aristocracy.

A livelihood had somehow to be provided for the Christian leaders (under the bishops) in respect of these 'private churches'. The rich nobleman who had provided the church building clearly had an obligation to do this. Gradually the more ancient term of "priest" seems to have superseded either presbyter or deacon to refer to a deputy for the bishop, and such a person was therefore "appointed by" the secular lord, rather than 'called forth' by the community to whom he would minister. This method of appointment was far removed from the collegiality of the leadership of the Early Church.

Rivalry ensued between the nobles and the clergy - a conflict between the secular power and the ecclesiastical power, in which the clergy established Ordination as a sacred rite independent of the whole ecclesia. At the third Lateran Council in 1179, interpretation was subtly varied to imply that instead of a call from a congregation, no one should be ordained without the assurance of a proper living! This accorded well with the "private church" concept: a livelihood for the appointed priest was easily provided by the 'Glebe', which furnished him with land to support himself in the same way as his parishoners did.

Before the era of financial investments or pension funds, this was probably the simplest provision that could be made. It developed into the 'parson's freehold', granting the priest security of tenure for life.

A further shift of emphasis also strengthened the clergy *vis-a-vis* the secular power. In the Early Church it had been considered necessary to hold ecclesiastical office to preside in the leadership of the Church. At the Fourth Lateran Council in 1215, Canon 6 of the Council of Chalcedon, which required the calling of its Leader by and to a local Church, was revoked! In other words, whereas the Early Church said that its minister was called to *lead* the Christian Community, the medieaval Church declared that a priest was ordained so that he would be able to celebrate the Eucharist. Priesthood thus became defined in relation to the cult instead of to the community.

The distinguishing feature of Christianity which separated it from other religions in the Middle Ages, was its emphasis on morality. Moral teaching was the duty of the clergy, moral inspiration the main object of its services and moral behaviour a necessary condition for receiving Holy Communion. Excommunication was therefore a very serious measure. Before the excommunicated person could be readmitted to communion he was required to appear publicly before the assembled Christians, with his head shaven, and to prostrate himself, to confess his sins, and implore absolution. This drastic measure, designed for moral discipline, could be adopted by clergy to strengthen their position vis-a-vis secular misbehaviour.

Hildebrand and the Papacy.

The Bishop of Rome had been accepted as preeminent from post-apostolic times. He had become rich and powerful. Hildebrand restored *authority* to the Papacy. He was first advisor to four Popes, then Pope himself (Gregory VII), 1073-1085. Bishops had become more than ecclesiastical officials; many had acquired power as landlords. The clergy was virtually the only educated class, and many bishops of those days corresponded to the senior civil servants of today. Hildebrand demanded that kings should relinquish the appointment of bishops in their territory to the Pope. The Emperor sought to depose the Pope; the Pope excommunicated the Emperor, whose temporal subjects rose against his government. The Emperor fled to face Hildebrand at Canossa, and (outwardly) capitulated.

There was nothing new in the Hildebrand philosophy; Christian virtues had been continually preached. The novel feature about this remarkable Pope was his courage in conducting a critical campaign against the widespread corruption of his time, both secular and among the clergy.

Out of the Hildebrand exercise of papal authority arose controversy that persists today. The more devoutly Christian party sets righteousness above material power; the imperialist argues the need for temporal authority in society. Hildebrand did not eliminate the corruption he perceived but it can be said that his attempt sowed seeds that germinated in the Reformation.

The controversies between Church and State, and between priests and people, stimulated intellectual activity, especially in theology and law, which encouraged the development of universities in all countries of Christendom.

From Hildebrand to the Reformation, three other major influences on Christianity must not be overlooked, *viz:* the Crusades, the Black Death and, above all, the introduction of printing to Europe. These, in quite different ways, had enormous consequences for the development of the Church.

The Crusades.

Various motives led to the Crusades. Norman freebooters welcomed a new opportunity for plunder; the rising ports of Venice and Genoa wanted to develop trade with the East; the western Latin Church saw a possible opportunity to dominate the Byzantine Church; and perhaps the most significant reason of all was the social disorganisation in Central Europe due to the extensive famine and pestilence that had prevailed there in 1094 and 1095. The most remarkable feature of this extraordinary episode of history was the sudden Will (or perhaps "submissive willingness" would be more correct) on the part of so many downcast, half-starving people to embark on such a strange adventure.

Details are in the history books, but the clergy of Europe cannot be exonerated for arousing religious fervour that misled many simple people and children. The Crusades gave rise to far more suffering and misery than romantic glory, and the Church lost much respect in consequence.

The Black Death (or The Great Pestilence)

A severe pandemic of plague started from Central Asia in the middle of the 14th century and transmitted by rat fleas, it spread across Europe and reduced the population by a about quarter in less than five years, with devastating social consequences. During the century or two prior to the pandemic, there had been a gradual but substantial increase in the population of Europe: "a vast increase in the western population in the eleventh and twelfth centuries with consequent land-hunger." (Paul Johnson). The exact proportion of this population increase can only be conjectured, and historians are not all agreed, but the consequence was that an excess of serfs became available, which provided the unskilled physical labour under the direction of master-masons to build the magnificent Gothic cathedrals in western Europe in the eleventh, twelfth and thirteenth centuries. Arthur Bryant has described this phenomenon: "It remains man's greatest achievement on earth. Even in our age of vast machines and scientific wonders, the Gothic cathedrals still stand as the greatest works we men have ever made...the Christian Faith has been the greatest continuing germinator of human energy at all levels of which there is any record in the annals of man."[2]

After it was all over, William of Wykeham founded a college at Winchester in 1382, the object of which was to educate priests to replace those lost during the Black Death. The Church had learned the importance of education among its clergy, because by this time they had become *the* educated people in society.

The Arrival of Printing in Europe.

Just as writing had transformed mankind's status in

the world almost three thousand years earlier by making it possible to communicate, not merely by speech to a companion, but by inscribing characters that could communicate the thought of one period to another period even centuries later, so printing made it possible to communicate not only with persons yet unborn, but to innumerable contemporary people whether near or far. Printing became practicable as soon as cheap paper became available on which thought and ideas could be represented in symbols. Gutenberg is generally credited with making this leap forward in Europe about 1460.

All this was of immediate consequence to the educated class (ie the clergy) by making the censorship of knowledge much more difficult, because previously uneducated people began to learn to read. Religious knowledge became available at far lower cost to far more people as a result of Bibles being abundantly printed. Common man progressively set up the Bible as a religious authority to counter-balance the tradition of the Church as expressed through its clergy. Such opportunity naturally led to intellectual development and critical discussion in society, especially in the universities, and this, not surprisingly, led to reform of the Medieaval Church.

References

E.W. Barnes *Rise of Christianity* (Longman Greene) 1947

H. Bettenson *Documents of the Christian Church* (O.U.P.) 1943

P. Johnson "History of Christianity" Pelican, 1976

E. Schillebeeck " 'Ministry' a case for change" SCM, 1981

D. C. Somerville "A short History of our Religion" G. Bell & Sons 1922

A. Bryant "The Lion and the Unicorn" Collins, 1969

The Reformation of The Church

Many English people regard the Reformation as the origin of the Church of England, an event instigated by Henry VIII when he seized the monasteries. However, the Reformation of the Church is a much wider process which cannot be so precisely dated.

It has already been suggested that the seeds of the Reformation were sown by Hildebrand. It can be further argued that some of these seeds tried to germinate in various movements during the later Middle Ages: for instance, the Waldensians in the Rhone valley (c. 1175), the Albigensian Crusade in France (c. 1208), the Lollards in England (c. 1380), or the Hussites in Bohemia (c. 1410). Nor was the Reformation a sudden event which happened when Luther nailed his theses to the Wittenburg Castle church door in 1517. Dissatisfaction with the way the Church was organised had been growing steadily during the later Middle Ages for various reasons, some of which have been referred to. Sooner or later some sort of change was inevitable, and it came with the arrival of printing.

Erasmus. (c. 1466 - 1536)

Erasmus was the first great Christian thinker and writer to be able to take advantage of the printing press to make his ideas widely known. He could be regarded as the "father of journalism" because he was the first to perceive the enormous influence and power of printing. His books were best-sellers across Europe for several years.

Surprisingly, he somehow avoided seizure, imprisonment, excommunication or even worse."

Erasmus was the illegitimate son of a priest, born in Holland about 1466, and as was then common, he had little option but to become a priest himself (1492). He was exceedingly fortunate in making influential friends and patrons, and this enabled him to visit England in 1498, where he was greatly influenced by hearing John Colet lecture in Oxford on St Paul's Epistle to the Romans. It appears that this experience led him to writing serious theology, pleading for a return to the source of Christianity in its primitive simplicity. He simply put the complicated dogma and ceremonial on one side, deeming them irrelevant, and interpreted Christianity directly from the Bible and the Patristic Fathers. He learned Greek and made a translation of the New Testament directly from the Greek into Latin. This ran to 300,000 copies which rapidly spread all over Europe.Through his writing and scholarship Erasmus immediately reached the attention of the best minds in Europe and became its foremost scholar for at least the decade 1510 - 1520. *In praise of folly,* his best known work, which satirizes princes and prelates, ran to thirty-nine editions, just one of which comprised 24,000 copies.

He avoided siding with Luther; he also tried to avoid opposing Luther, although his support was sought by both sides. In adopting this *via media* he undoubtedly gained wide support from those who recognised the need for sensible reform of the Church, but wished to achieve this reasonably and without violence.In contrast to the medieval sacerdotalism, Erasmus did not believe in an exclusive role for the clergy and welcomed the widening of the educated classes to include more laity. This meant that more and more people became literate and so were able to read the Bible, which diminished the significance of the clergy's insistence that only they could interpret the scriptures correctly. (Hitherto, even the mere scrutiny of the Bible by a layman had sometimes been considered presumptive of heresy.) Erasmus was certainly in full accord with the Reformation view that the Scriptures provide the best authority of the Christian religion, rather than the alleged "tradition" passed down by the clergy.

In contrast to the "authority of the Church", which concept had been so dear to St Augustine, Erasmus argued that Christianity was based on the straightforward virtues taught by Jesus Christ in the New Testament, and that reform of the Church meant a recognition of His authority. (Erasmus died in 1536, the year in which a copy of the Bible became statutory furnishing in the Church of England.)

Thus the central question regarding the Christian Reformation became a matter of the relative merit of the authority of the Church vis-a-vis the authority of the Scriptures. Neither attitude is as clear-cut as one might expect. Herein lies the profound controversy which began at the time of the Reformation and still continues.

Martin Luther. (1483 - 1546)

Luther is still a controversial figure in the history of the Church. Tradition has it that he first became prominent in the direction of ecclesiastical reform by nailing ninety-five arguments against "indulgences" on the Church door of Wittenburg Castle on October 31st 1517. An 'indulgence' enabled the purchaser to obtain remission of time to be spent in purgatory after death, by payment in cash during life. A Dominican monk, John Tetzel, had been selling these to raise money, ostensibly for the rebuilding of St Peter's Basilica in Rome, but just possibly for other more local purposes.The angry professor at Wittenburg University almost certainly wrote to both his prince and his bishop in protest, and it is reasonably certain that thanks to the printing press his arguments were being circulated all over Germany by the end of 1517, and not only in Latin, but in German as well. There was already irritation regarding the moral integrity of the Church and pressure to raise money for the Pope in Rome was widely detested by the princes in Europe. So the moral protest by a priest (Luther was ordained in 1507) was immediately popular.

It would be quite wrong to think of Luther's protest as impetuous. His academic ability had been recognised from 1502; he renounced a career in law in 1505 and entered a strict Augustinian Monastery. It seems that at this time, like Saul the Pharisee (St Paul), he believed that Salvation was to be obtained by meticulous effort - salvation by works. In 1510 he was sent to visit Rome on monastic business and was deeply troubled by the moral laxity he found prevalent there (curiosity, doubt?). Two years later, meditating privately in his cell, he was inspired by reading Romans (Ch. 1, 16 - 17), perceiving that Salvation was attained not by doing good works but by faith in a gracious God (explanation). The similarity of this insight to St Paul's experience to the

Damascus road is obvious, and it immediately modified Luther's professorial teaching (acceptance?), though the wide publicity only arose from his protest in 1517 (commitment). At once he became the focal point of protest against the Papacy which, after more than two years of argument, culminated in Luther's excommunication in 1520.

But the indulgence issue was merely the tinder that lit the fire. It suited very well the interests of the secular princes of Europe, who were exasperated by the wheedling of wealth from western Europe to enrich the Vatican coffers. So, by his public moral action Luther attracted both princely support and Papal condemnation.

Luther rejected the sacerdotal concept of the clergy as a priestly caste: "baptism, gospel and faith, these alone suffice to create a Christian People." [1.] This is the kernel of the Protestant Reformation: good works are not a precondition for the Christian faith, but *the result of it:* "By their fruits ye shall know them" (Matt. Ch. 7, 20). Such emphasis differs sharply from the medieval concept of the ecclesiastical power presiding over the *corpus mysticum Christi* and the revocation of Canon 6 of the Declaration of Chalcedon at the Lateran Council of 1215.

Luther would have probably been content with that much reformation without any more precise interpretation of the *Corpus Mysticum Christi* but Ulrich Zwingli (1481 - 1531) was more radical, protesting that the Mass was no more than a memorial meal. Such a view necessarily differed drastically from the accepted concept of the celebration of the Eucharist as a ritual only possible by an ordained priest.

Zwingli's early death, and the eclipse of Luther, brought John Calvin to pre-eminence in the Reforming movement.

John Calvin. (1509 - 1564)

Calvin was born in northern France.His father, a lawyer, intended him for the Church and as a young man he served a chaplaincy, but he then resolved against taking Holy Orders. From study of the Scriptures he inclined toward the Reformed Faith: "God, by a sudden conversion subdued and brought my mind to a teachable frame". By an almost chance diversion from Strasburg, he first came to Geneva in 1536. At that time Geneva was an independent city of the Empire; the Town Council had expelled its bishop and adopted Protestantism. Calvin was attracted by the opportunity of creating there a religious unit of society which, he believed, would resemble the primitive Church.

How John Calvin won and then retained the confidence of 13,000 inhabitants of Geneva for more than twenty years is not clear. Calvinism was 'democratic' in the sense that the community was governed by a Council, but this Council seems to have been totally under the domination of Calvin. Public worship was compulsory; gaily coloured clothes and dancing were forbidden; unchastity was sometimes punished by death. The Eucharist was a solemn privilege from which moral offenders were punished by excommunication.

Calvin certainly held the Lutheran doctrine of Justification by Faith, but he also held the strange doctrine of

Predestination: "Men are not created on an equal footing; for some, eternal life is preordained; for others eternal damnation."[2] Calvin derived this doctrine from St Augustine: "Will any man presume to say that God did not foreknow those to whom he would grant belief ...?"[3] This whole idea of predestination, on the correct understanding of which theologians are at variance, should be compared with St Paul's difficult passage in Rom. Ch. 9, from which argument it is derived (see page 62).

However, suffice it here to say that Calvin's teaching on predestination has undoubtedly led to energetic religious conviction and rigid ethical behaviour in the several branches of the Church that he influenced, which included not only the early English Puritans, but also those other Puritans who emigrated to New England.

On the continent of Europe the Reformation began as a religious movement, Erasmus expressing a form of Christian humanism, Luther a moral indignation and salvation through faith, and Calvin a rigid moral imposition in Geneva.

The unity of medieval Catholicism was severely disturbed; but by the Protestant acknowledgement of the authority of Scripture, Protestantism was to split up into many divisions, because it allowed for the perception of new religious truth as understanding of the Scriptures increased and the whole field of human knowledge expanded.

The English Reformation.

In England, the Reformation began as a political rather than a religious movement. The government's financial difficulties, the dissolution of the rich monasteries, the Royal Divorce, and the usurpation of sovereignty over the Church of England in 1534, were related issues. The result did separate the Church of England from the Papacy, while attempting to retain the Catholic Faith with some Reforming concessions. However, under the Sovereign instead of the Pope, the Church of England became a "via media", as it were, attempting to ride two horses simultaneously round the circus ring! (And, it must be admitted, not unsuccessfully!) The Tudor monarchs trod a delicate path, but by the time Queen Elizabeth I was excommunicated in 1570, the Church of England had become a separate branch of the Christian Church.

Its more conservative Catholic wing and its more radical Protestant wing were held together not by doctrine but by the shrewd political skill of the Tudor sovereigns and their advisers and also the solemn beauty of the vernacular English liturgy constructed by its leading churchmen.

The concept of a personal religion: "as a man thinketh in his heart, so is he" (Prov. Ch. 23, 7) did not reach the religious thought of ordinary people until more than a century later. Democracy spread a little, partly influenced by Calvin. Common man's understanding of the Bible was enhanced by the spread of printing, and because more and more people learned to read the range of human knowledge extended enormously, as scholarship increased and the Renaissance unfolded during this period.

The Counter-Reformation.

Although Luther's protest was in 1517, no rapprochement between the Reformers and the Papacy occurred during the next twenty years. Disease, war, and social turmoil had disrupted western Europe, while the Emperor's battles to repel Islam had disrupted eastern Europe.

During this period of religious rethinking, reconciliation between the Papacy and the Lutherans failed at the Diet of Ratisbon in 1541, and Paul IV (1555 - 59) attempted to suppress reformed thinking through censorship and the Papal Inquisition - but this had become impossible. (The history of Christianity has been sullied by attempts to suppress unorthodox belief ever since the Marcion heresy).

However, in 1540 Ignatius Loyola and nine friends offered unconditional obedience to the Pope, who ordained them priests and allowed them to form the Society of Jesus (Jesuits). Their Papal allegiance was strict and unquestioning. They attempted to overthrow Protestantism by devious paths (which included attempted assassination). They invented the system of casuistry by classifying the degree of various human sins and then, as Confessors, made the penitents feel that their sins were less serious than might be expected. Thus they acquired knowledge of important secrets!

In 1545 the Pope convened the Council of Trent, which was dominated by the Jesuits. Hostile to the reformers, it attempted to define the doctrines of the Church, condemning Justification by Faith by simply declaring that Statements of the Pope were equal to the

Bible in importance; and rejecting the Hussite claim that laity should receive the Chalice at Communion. The Council of Trent also set up the famous 'index' of books which Catholic laity were forbidden to read! It finally concluded in 1563.

However, the most constructive outcome of the Counter-Reformation was probably the Jesuit emphasis on education, as a result of which education has undoubtedly exerted a considerable influence on society ever since. Unfortunately, differences between Catholics and Reformers became polarised to an extent that has persisted even into the twentieth century.

References.

1. *Appeal to The German Ruling Classes* Tony Lane in *Christian Thought* (Lion Books) p.117
2. *Institutes of The Christian Religion* Bk III, xxi, quoted in *Documents of the Christian Church* Bettenson, (O.U.P.), 1943, p.300
3. *De Dono* St Augustine, quoted in op. cit. p.80
4. *A History of Europe* H.A.L. Fisher, (Arnold), 1936
5. *A History of Christianity* Paul Johnson, Pelican, 1976
6. *A Short History of Our Religion* D.C. Somervell, (Bell & Sons) London, 1922

THE SIGNIFICANCE OF JOHN AND CHARLES WESLEY

It is not possible to understand the influence of John and Charles Wesley on Christianity in England without some understanding of the state of the English Church of that period. John Wesley was unquestionably the most significant religious figure in Britain during the eighteenth century and by the beginning of the twentieth century, Methodism, with an estimated world membership of thirty million, had become the largest Protestant Church denomination in the world. Yet neither brother ever left, or was excluded from, the Church of England.

John Wesley's religious genius cannot be properly realised without understanding the talents of his brother Charles, or the shrewd wisdom of his mother, Susannah Wesley. John's intellectual ability, his prolific authorship, his remarkable flair for organisation, his stamina for travel (usually on horseback), and his ineptitude with women were all facets in his extraordinary ministry.

The Family Background.

The family was well-connected though relatively poor. Both sons, and their father Samuel Wesley, were graduates of Oxford University. John Wesley's position as a Fellow of Lincoln College for about twenty years established his academic status and provided a base for his literary livelihood. Grandfather John Wesley was a clergyman in Dorset, while grandfather Samuel Annersley was a non-juror in 1688.

Great-grandfather Bartholomew Wesley ministered in Dorset but was ejected under the Act of Uniformity in 1662. (Perhaps he deserved this because he almost caught King Charles II fleeing across Dorset after his defeat at the battle of Worcester.) Great-grandfather John White was vicar of Dorchester, and is remembered for enabling a group of his people to sail as pilgrims to Massachusetts in 1635, where they founded the town of Dorchester (now a suburb of Boston). Another Great-Grandfather, also a John White, sat in the Long Parliament which sentenced Charles I to death. Bartholomew Wesley's parents, Sir Herbert and his wife Elizabeth de Wellesley, each inherited large estates, mainly in Ireland.

When Charles Wesley was Head Boy at Westminster School, Garrett Wesley, a kinsman in Ireland (descended from Sir Herbert and Elizabeth), who was a wealthy landowner, but without an heir, wrote to Charles' father, the Rev. Samuel Wesley, offering to adopt the boy and bring him up to inherit the extensive property. Samuel left the decision to his son. Charles preferred to take up his newly awarded scholarship to Christchurch, Oxford, and so Garrett Wesley adopted a different kinsman instead: Richard, the son of Sir Charles Colley, who became the grandfather of Richard, Marquis of Wellesley and his brother the Duke of Wellington. Thus Charles' decision to go to Oxford had momentous military and political as well as religious consequences for British history.

At Oxford Charles gathered friends round him who practised their religion seriously, taking communion regularly and visiting the sick and those in prison. John,

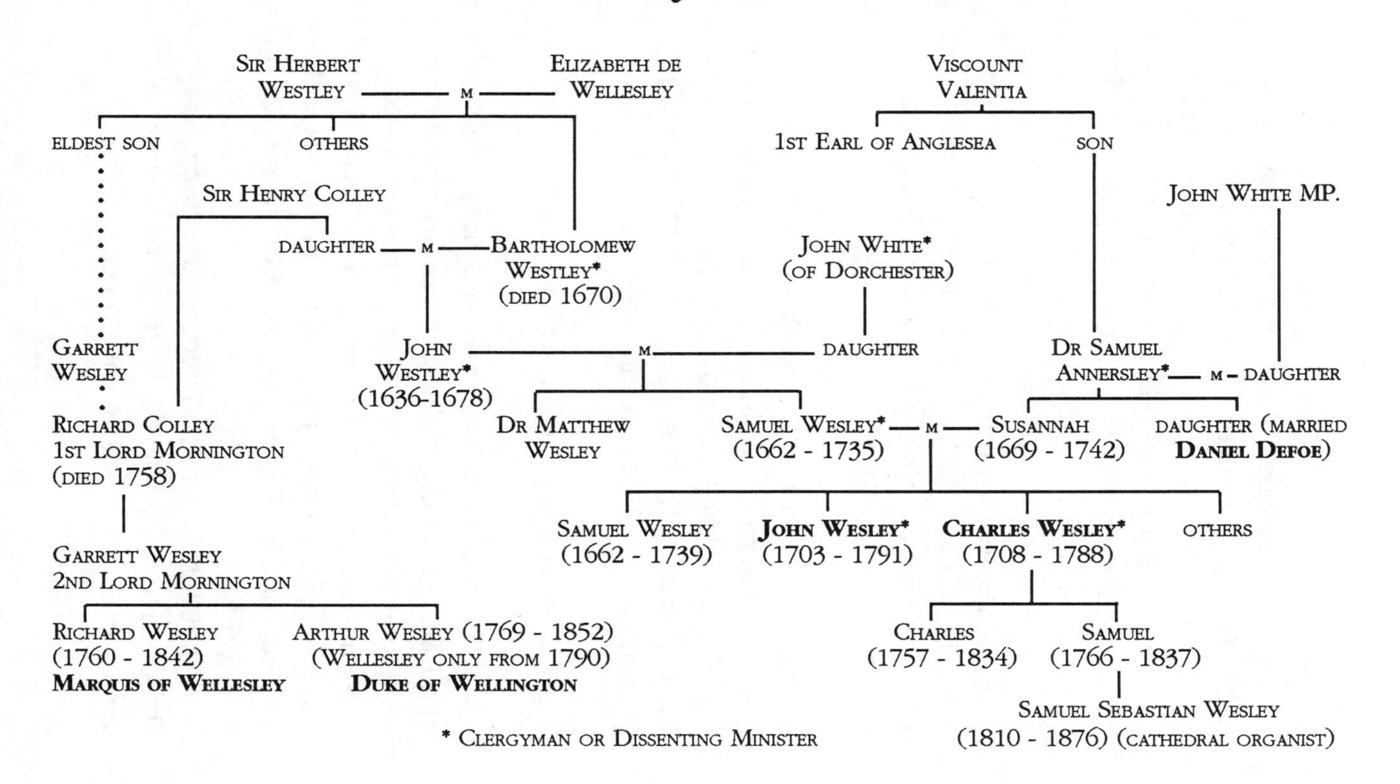
The Ancestry of John and Charles Wesley
Sir Herbert Westley
m
Elizabeth de Wellesley
Viscount Valentia
eldest son
others
1st Earl of Anglesea
son
Sir Henry Colley
John White MP.
daughter
m
Bartholomew Westley*
(died 1670)
John White*
(of Dorchester)
Garrett Wesley
John Westley*
(1636-1678)
m
daughter
Dr Samuel Annersley*
m
daughter
Richard Colley
1st Lord Mornington
(died 1758)
Dr Matthew Wesley
Samuel Wesley*
(1662 - 1735)
m
Susannah
(1669 - 1742)
daughter (married
Daniel Defoe)
Samuel Wesley
(1662 - 1739)
John Wesley*
(1703 - 1791)
Charles Wesley*
(1708 - 1788)
others
Garrett Wesley
2nd Lord Mornington
Richard Wesley
(1760 - 1842)
Marquis of Wellesley
Arthur Wesley (1769 - 1852)
(Wellesley only from 1790)
Duke of Wellington
Charles
(1757 - 1834)
Samuel
(1766 - 1837)
Samuel Sebastian Wesley
(1810 - 1876) (cathedral organist)
* Clergyman or Dissenting Minister

by now a Fellow of Lincoln College, became the leader of this informal group, which acquired the nickname 'methodist'. Both young men at this time experienced a period of heart-searching (curiosity?) after spiritual certainty. They later even went to Georgia as missionaries but made no impact whatever, returning in greater spiritual uncertainty than before. Then on Whitsunday 1738, first Charles, and on the following Wednesday, John, each quite independently underwent a profound religious experience. John wrote in his journal: "... I felt my heart strangely warmed; I felt that I did trust in God alone for salvation ..." ("explanation" or "acceptance").

The details of John Wesley's Conversion are remarkably described in his Journal (Vol I, pp.96 ff). These follow the pattern of well-known conversion experiences and the underlying psychological principles indicated in the earlier chapter on religious conversion (curiosity, explanation, acceptance, commitment).

Eighteenth Century English Religion.

The state of religion and morality in England were at a low level in the eighteenth century and this was undoubtedly relevant to the religious revival. Absentee clergymen were commonplace (yet still 4,000 clergy to 11,000 parishes!); candidates for Ordination were scandalously ignorant of the Bible and lax in parochial responsibilities afterwards.

Drinking spirits had become a national habit within the previous fifty years (a social phenomenon comparable to smoking in the twentieth century) and three Acts of Parliament had failed to alter it. One in six London shops was a 'grog shop'. "Drunk for a penny, dead drunk for tuppence." was a common slogan. English politics were corrupt and bribery was widespread. Indifference toward poverty abounded; smuggling and wreck plundering around the coast were normal; slavery, the press gang and child labour were the accepted order of the day.

In any consideration of today's modern social problems, it is wise to remember the state of English society in which John and Charles Wesley lived less than three hundred years ago, because the moral climate has changed so much for the better, and their influence played a large part in effecting this.

The Wesleyan Revival Begins.

Religious conversion leads to action. On New Years Day 1739 the Wesleys, together with some sixty friends, held a love-feast, and this marked the real beginning of the extraordinary religious revival in England.

They began preaching to various religious meetings; when persons were thus 'converted', sometimes in what seemed almost a hysterical fit (curiosity plus emotion), Wesley organised them into little groups for instruction (explanation), which enabled them to continue building up their religious experience. (This discipline remained the focal point of good Methodist practice into the twentieth century.) As these little 'societies' grew, Wesley divided them up into 'classes', each with a Class Leader, and membership was recognised by the issue of a Class

Ticket. Both Wesleys and their friends travelled the countryside preaching, and thus the movement grew - and it grew very rapidly.

The religious doctrine of the societies was that of the Church of England: "A serious clergyman desired to know in what point we differed from the Church of England. I answered, "To the best of my knowledge in none; the doctrines we preach are the fundamental doctrines of the Church clearly laid down in her prayers, articles and homilies." (John Wesley's Journal, 13.9.1739)

What are, or were, these "fundamental doctrines" in eighteenth century England? Anyone who has read the *Forty-four sermons of John Wesley,* which to this day are the doctrinal basis of Methodism, will certainly conclude that they comprise straightforward Christianity. Two doctrines are alleged to have been especially emphasised in Wesleyan preaching:

Firstly, the Doctrine of Scriptural Holiness, or Christian Perfection: "Be ye therefore perfect even as your heavenly Father is perfect" (Matt. Ch. 5, 48), insisting that no limits can be set to the sovereign love of God. *Perfect love* destroys the distinction between secular and sacred things: all life is sanctified in Christ and there is no holiness but social holiness.

Secondly, the Doctrine of Assurance refers to that inner conviction that each of us is accepted by God for what we are. It is a relationship of love comparable with a little child knowing that he is loved by his parents, or perhaps better expressed as "falling in love"; but attested to, not by intensity of emotion, but by "the fruits of the spirit" in daily living. Both these doctrines are characteristics of Christian experience down the ages.

Before the Reformation it can be said that in European feudal society men and women sought salvation via "the Church". The Reformation under Luther at first put the emphasis on to individual religion, but somehow the Calvinist influence switched the "authority of the Church" to the "authority of the Bible." The Wesleyan movement switched the emphasis back to individual religion again, but avoided the risk of personal isolation by insistence on corporate class meetings and regular worship.

Like any new movement of the human spirit, expansion required finance. At first John Wesley raised this by his own writings. His books and pamphlets brought him a big income, all of which he gave away. Soon, however, every class member contributed a penny per week. The class leaders collected this and they often made good from their own pockets when a member was ill or fell on hard times.

The class members were instructed to seek Holy Communion in their parish churches regularly, but there were practical difficulties. Industrial expansion had led to population growth in areas often remote from existing churches and many of these new industrial populations knew nothing of religion at all! *It was these people in their many thousands, rather than church people,* who were converted to a warm and vigorous Christianity by the Wesleyan movement. In many areas only open-air preaching was legally possible, which both John and Charles were reluctant to adopt. Their Mother, Susannah Wesley, urged them to reconsider. Wesley had very few Ordained clergy to help him, and again it was Susannah who advised the use of laymen.

In many parishes Wesley's followers were unacceptable to the country parsons and to the gentry who had appointed them. These were often uneasy about preaching serious Christianity to the lower social classes. Perhaps it was an unconscious expression of that innate primitive *fear* which it was Jesus' purpose to overcome. Because Wesley's followers were so often rebuffed they built their own chapels, and reluctantly Wesley had to concede permission for Holy Communion to be celebrated there - but only after they had been rejected at their parish church. Not until 1836 were the parish boundaries revised, and by then strong Methodist Societies were established in many places where previously there had been no parish church.

Such was the vigour of early Wesleyanism, and its message cannot be better summarised than in words from Wesley's own *Earnest Appeal to Men of Reason:* "... we see on every side either men of no religion at all or men of a lifeless formal religion. We are grieved by the sight and should rejoice if by any means we might convince some that there is a better religion to be obtained, a religion worthy of God that gave it. And this we conceive to be no other than Love; the love of God and all mankind, the loving God with all our heart and of life ..."

Sequelae to the Wesleyan Revival.

After Wesley's death in 1791, as has happened so very many times in Christian history, the movement divided. Those already accepted within the established

Church simply developed Wesleyan practice as it appeared to them, but they remained within the parent Church of England. They were, on the whole, rich and influential people who became an important pressure group among the gentility of that church, and within which the Clapham Sect, under the powerful influence of William Wilberforce, was outstanding as a political and Christian force, at the forefront of much reform.

The poorer wage-earners, whom Wesley had brought to Christianity largely from a non-religious background, understandably remained outside the established church. This was partly because they were legally required to licence their 'chapels', which made them technically into dissenters. Celebration of Holy Communion was discouraged in their chapels, and they were expected to attend their parish churches for communion. Thus they gradually drifted away from the Church, though some societies refrained from celebration of Holy Communion as late as 1870, although their baptisms, marriages and funerals were usually conducted in the parish churches. Methodist Preachers did not adopt the title Reverend until 1818, and there were no Methodist 'Ordinations' in England until 1836, ie. forty-five years after John Wesley's death.

Wesley's Ordinations.

It is worthwhile to recapitulate the story of John Wesley's American Ordinations because today there are approximately four times as many Methodists in the United States (12 million) as there are Episcopalians (Anglicans) (3 million). A.B. Lawson deals with this subject in his book

John Wesley and the Christian Ministry.

Neither Wesley, nor Methodism since, has ever opposed episcopacy as a method of church government, but Methodism holds that a mechanical doctrine of unbroken succession by Ordination from the Apostles themselves, is both historically and theologically vulnerable.

The ecclesiastical predicament in September 1783, at the end of the American War of Independence, found the newly independent colonies exhausted, bankrupt and without any proper ministry from the Church of England. So in May 1784 Wesley consulted the Bishop of London about consecrating a bishop. The Bishop declined; as an English bishop he was uncertain of his status in relation to the now independent rebels; but it was because Dr Lowth was a bishop that Wesley reiterated his request in June 1784, again unsuccessfully.

Under pressure from Methodists in America, in September 1784 Wesley with two other Anglican presbyters, "laid hands" on five preachers that they might "go and superintend" the Methodist societies in the ex-colonies.

Simultaneously, but unknown to Wesley, disheartened churchmen in the United States selected the Rev. Samuel Seabright from among their few clergymen and sent him to England to beg for Consecration. The See of Canterbury was vacant. The Archbishop of York declined to consecrate Seabright; but the two Bishops of Aberdeen and Ross & Moray did consecrate him on Nov. 17th, just ten weeks after Wesley's 'Ordinations'.

If at this time the English bishops had consented to ordain even a few Methodist preachers, the whole Connexion could have undoubtedly remained within the

Church of England.

The Nineteeth Century.

Throughout the nineteenth century Methodism was vigorous and schismatic, philanthropic and missionary, financially independent and expanding all over the world, so that by the beginning of the twentieth century it exerted an enormous religious and social influence. Teetotalism (from 1833) developed from Wesley's preaching against gin drinking and the distilling of spirits (although ale brewing was taught in Methodist classes); the Tolpuddle Martyrs (1836), who formed an early 'trade union' movement, were Methodist local preachers; William Booth left the Methodist ministry to found the Salvation Army (1878). But the most significant consequence of the Wesleyan Revival was the renewal of Christian spirituality all across England, and not only within Methodism. This revival influenced very many thousands of laymen, but involved relatively few Church of England clergy. Consequently, many men and women learned to share in the government not only of the Methodist Connexion, but to participate increasingly in local government. This raised the moral standard of national and local politics and became associated with the rise of first the liberal, and later the socialist political parties.

Lay participation in church affairs was looked askance at by the clergy, and lower class participation in politics was disapproved of by the aristocracy and gentry. Nevertheless, even today British politics is influenced by the Wesleyan movement, and both wings of the Anglican

Church owe much to the inspiration of John and Charles Wesley.

References.

Robert Southey's *Life of John Wesley* 1820

Telford, J. *Life of John Wesley* (Epworth Press) 1899

Edwards, M. *John Wesley and The Eighteenth Century* (Epworth Press) 1955

Journal of John Wesley (four vols.), Everyman Library, (J.M. Dent)

Lawson, A.B. *John Wesley and The Christian Ministry* (S.P.C.K.) 1963

Townsend, Workman and Eayrs *A New History of Methodism* Hodder & Stoughton 1909

Ethics

Religion, Custom & Law.

There is undoubtedly a relationship between religion, custom and law; but that relationship is by no means clearly defined. Many people hold that the word "religion" implies a belief in some kind of a superhuman power - a God - to be obeyed and worshipped in some form of ritual, and that this in some way shapes the course of human existence; a bond or knot of some kind between man and God. Other people would insist that any systematised belief or ethic constitutes a religion. So it is wise to acknowledge straight away that men and women do not agree precisely what religion means.

The word 'custom' is often used to describe any habitual practice of either individual behaviour, or the behaviour pattern of a particular social group, eg. sleeping with a spear close to hand, scattering entrails to divine the future, going to church regularly on Sunday, or shutting the pub promptly at closing time. It does not follow that we all agree exactly on the meaning of custom.

Law' expresses a code of behaviour which one particular unit of society endeavours to enforce by its own established authority. Another unit of society may have a different law. Again, therefore, it does not follow that there would be precise agreement on the meaning of law.

Morality.

Consideration of these three suggested meanings illustrates how varied they may be, but the uncertainties are multiplied if 'morality' is also introduced - defined (by Collins Dictionary) as "being in accord with the principles of right and wrong in conduct." The various patterns and principles of morality are systematised under the term 'Ethics.

It is very difficult to clarify just how Religion, Custom, Law and Morality inter-relate - so quite arbitrarily, I shall use these terms loosely and from what I personally believe to be a Christian point of view. We are seeking rules for human behaviour and, in particular, rules for Christian behaviour. Several different ethical yardsticks may be chosen by different people on different occasions.

Absolute Codes.

Perhaps the best known system is 'The Ten Commandments'. These seem to lay down clear guidance - but do they? For instance: "Thou shalt not kill." (Ex. Ch. 20, 13, or Deut. Ch. 5, 17). Nothing could be more succinct; but is there not some difference between shooting men in warfare, murdering someone in passion, destroying an unborn baby, or killing an animal to eat it? Or quite accidentally killing a player in a cricket or football match (as happens occasionally), or when driving a car when there is perhaps a touch of ice on the road, or a touch of alcohol in the body? What *exactly* is the *moral* difference between these? One could ask similar questions about the meanings of prostitution, fornication, adultery and marriage. One could get into similar difficulties with stealing, borrowing and shop-lifting. The point is that there are often grey areas about which juries and even learned judges will sometimes differ. So although absolute codes may seem clear and attractive, they are not always straightforward. Similar difficulties arise regarding the authority of other absolute codes, eg. the Hippocratic Oath, the Geneva Convention, or the Helsinki Declaration of Human Rights.

Conscience.

Few people would deny that everyone seems to have some sort of conscience - some more sensitive than others. Our Quaker friends attach great importance to that Still, Small Voice for guidance; but how reliable is it? At least two great philosophers, Hobbes and Locke, both rejected the existence of conscience, declaring it to be the same as a man's judgement of a situation. If God has given mankind some degree of freedom of choice (independent judgement) besides a conscience, is that hair-splitting or not? About a hundred years ago Sigmund Freud discovered that we have a subconscious mind that does most of our thinking, most of its processes never reaching the surface of conscious thought. Freud showed that early relationships with parents have much to do with the development of conscience from infancy onward. The difficulty in evaluating our conscience is greatly increased when one person has the responsibility of decision but another has the responsibility of implementation: eg. the minority view of the conscientious objector to war, or the house physician advised by an experienced consultant to carry out a form of treatment with which the younger, less experienced colleague sincerely disagrees.

Utilitarianism.

This is a system of ethics advocated by Jeremy Bentham and John Stuart Mill in the nineteenth century. It recommends that when a choice of conduct is difficult, one should prefer that line of conduct which will provide the greatest happiness for the largest number of persons. I have often taken refuge in this ethic! During a winter epidemic, a hospital may find itself desperately short of staff because nurses are off sick; but at the same time there is often a surge in requests for admission because many of the public are also sick. In such a situation I have authorised the temporary closure of hospital wards that cannot be adequately staffed, so that those patients already in hospital can be properly looked after.

Many decisions in politics reflect this principle. In a democracy it can be argued that this is merely vote-catching! Stalin applied it in the 1930s to liquidate many thousands of farm-workers. I certainly would not choose it to justify euthanasia for an elderly patient who had become a burden to his family! There are two flaws regarding utilitarianism: firstly, it is quantitative, implying that right and wrong can be influenced by numbers. Secondly it equates morality with happiness. But they are not equivalent.

The Natural Law.

The Christian Church has often opted to be guided by 'Natural Law'. It is well expressed in Stoicism, and spelt out by Seneca, Epictitus and Marcus Aurelius among others - all 'good' men. Natural Law simply argues that *Good* is to be done, while *Evil* is to be avoided, and it postulates that Mankind can discern the difference by the exercise of his Reason, which enables him to perceive what is right and rational, and to disregard any considerations influenced by emotion or desire.

Is mankind such a rational being? I doubt it. Thomas Aquinas postulated that the Catholic Church could competently arbitrate regarding any difficult situation. However, many of us would not accept a third party as referee, preferring our own Reason as arbiter. (Is this simply a Protestant subterfuge?)

Duty.

Acknowledging this difficulty, in the eighteenth century Emmanuel Kant attempted to clarify the dilemma by developing the notion of 'duty': doing what should be done regardless of personal feeling or consequence. Duty may help us to get up immediately the alarm clock rings on a cold day (it is my duty to rise), or to make a heroic dash on the battlefield (which may win a V.C.), but it does not seem to me specially helpful in sorting out personal or emotional dilemmas concerning right or wrong. The root idea of duty is to serve or give something in return for something.

Casuistry.

The attempt to apply moral rules to particular circumstances (casuistry) can become very complicated and it comes close to valuing its principles more highly than it values the person they are applied to: (If *that* happens, then *this* is the judgement). Unless all the relevant parties share very close religious agreement, I doubt if such moral case-rules are helpful.

Situation Ethics.

In this century a system has developed that has won considerable support. Situation Ethics [1] puts love and compassion above all other considerations (you may find that reminds you of Christian teaching), and in consequence, it denies all absolute ethical standards, but puts *respect for persons* as its over-riding principle. It can be regarded as an attempt to create a system of casuistry which puts *love* as its first principle - which is an attractive idea!

For its purpose, a *person* is someone *with whom it is possible to communicate* (not necessarily by speech); and *respect* implies involvement with others such that *our own choices and intentions are influenced by their aims and aspirations as well as our own*. Furthermore, every moral situation has to be reasoned out on its own merits - which takes time.

This system has provided me with very acceptable guide-lines in many relationships with patients. One of its recognised weaknesses is that it sometimes conflicts with justice, which it tends to disregard, but so sometimes does

Christian forgiveness! John Robinson[2] has declared situation ethics "the only ethic for mankind come of age", while William Barclay has commented that "mankind has not yet come of age", and therefore declares that "mankind still needs the crutch and protection of the law"[3]. If we insist that in every situation every man must make his own decisions, then first, we must make every man morally and lovingly fit to take such decisions!

Peter Baelz[4] states a more academic criticism of situation ethics and - as I understand him - criticizes it mainly on the grounds that it fails to come to terms with the concept of justice.

Comment.

Thus there are at least some half dozen ethical yardsticks which are widely recognised and used today. How are ordinary people to sort out their ethical problems? Part of the difficulty is undoubtedly that modern civilisation has brought about so many changes in Society, and so very rapidly, that we have just not had long enough to adjust to the consequences and implications of one drastic change before another one is upon us. The organisation of the Church seems to be too rigid. How can its teaching keep pace with today's rapidly changing world?

Modern Ethical Issues.

For instance, just over one hundred years ago, in 1877, Charles Bradlaugh and Annie Besant were sentenced to imprisonment for blasphemy (ie pornography). They had been distributing Dr Knowleton's pamphlet publicising birth control methods. It is reasonably certain that even fifty years ago, no medical school gave any sort of teaching on that subject; but about thirty years ago improved techniques made contraception more reliable, thus forcing a reconsideration of its moral implications. If there is a moral aspect to contraception, what guidance to it does the Church give us today?

In 1932 an eminent obstetrician, Alec Bourne, resolved to test the English legal attitude toward abortion. Having advised the police and invited prosecution he aborted 'unlawfully' and in a London teaching hospital a girl of fourteen who had been successively raped by three guardsmen (these facts were not in dispute). The legal question turned on the interpretation of "unlawful" and the court found that when a medical man was acting in the interest of his patient to preserve her life or health, there was no adverse criticism to offer. As a result of this interpretation, public opinion began to change.

Pacifism became an active ethical issue between the two world wars; yet already it has lost much of its relevance in view of the utter totality of any future world-scale war. The Church did not give any consistent guidance on the rights or wrongs of the pacifist position.

How do we determine an ethical attitude toward artificial insemination or genetic manipulation? Is an embryo really a 'person'? What exactly does "The Sanctity of Life" really mean? (see also page 177) There is a lot of imprecise thinking about this.

Can there be a Christian attitude to euthanasia? How should we express a Christian attitude towards world-scale pollution or care of the total environment?

We cannot just shrug off these problems. Surely an all-powerful Creator did not evolve the human race and give us the power of choice for us to ignore such moral issues? History is resplendent with great and good people who have given their whole lives and energy in the cause of bettering the world we live in. It is our Christian responsibility to wrestle with these issues.

The carpenter of Galilee was not just a friend to little children; he was not just a gentle Jesus meek and mild; he was not merely a mystical incarnation conceived by the Holy Ghost and born of the Virgin Mary. He was an extraordinary Person who taught some devastatingly new ideas about the Way to Live. "He was too great for His disciples to understand. The priests, rulers and rich men who were his enemies understood Him far more clearly, because they realised that there was no choice for them but to destroy Him if they were to prosper." So they did. (Wells). [5.]

The amazing thing is that two thousand years later, as a result of that Man's blazing light to the world, His way of life has been handed down to our generation and we accept the responsibility of applying His teaching to the problems of our own era to the utmost of our ability, which is by no means easy.

All ethical codes have their weaknesses and imperfections when we look to them for guidance regarding many current moral dilemmas. There is not just one "right" code of behaviour for many of the moral problems facing mankind today. If we as Christians are to fulfil our moral duty in good conscience, then we can only discern the right and wrong of a particular situation as expressed in the spirit of His Ministry as it is declared in the Sermon on the Mount - not just the Beatitudes, but right through to: *"FOR HE TAUGHT THEM AS ONE HAVING AUTHORITY AND NOT AS THE SCRIBES"* (Matt. Ch. 7, 29).

References.

1. Fletcher J. *Situation Ethics* S.C.M. Press 1966
2. Robinson J.A.T. *Honest to God* S.C.M. Press p. 117
3. Barclay W. *Ethics in a Permissive Society* p.81ff
4. Peter Baelz *Ethics and Belief* Sheldon Press London, 1977
5. Wells H.G. *Outline of History* Cassell & Co., 1920, p.531
6. Campbell A.V. *Moral Dilemmas in Medicine* Churchill Livingstone 1975

SCIENCE AND CHRISTIANITY

"Thousands of people today, believe that the historic faith in which our civilisation is rooted was discredited about one hundred and fifty years ago, and they have abandoned a religion about which they know little, at the behest of a science about which they probably know less." (Donald Hughes). [1.]

There have certainly been misunderstandings; it is therefore, important to know just what science is, and what Christianity is, too.

Science can be defined as systematised knowledge derived from observation, study and experimentation. It is important to understand this.

Modern science is essentially a *method* for acquiring measurable, factual knowledge. The discovery of the circulation of the blood by William Harvey (1578-1657) (published in 1628 as *De motu cordis*) serves as an excellent example.

Harvey had worked at Padua and would be aware of the hazards that Bruno and Galileo had encountered from the Church. He would be aware of the sacred significance of blood [2.] and the personal risk of promulgating heresy. Yet at the same time all sorts of fantastic notions about the function of the heart and blood vessels were prevalent. For instance: that the heart was the 'workshop' in which necessary 'spirits' were manufactured; or, that the arteries contained a mixture of blood and air; or that the septum dividing the heart was a fine sieve through which blood percolated from side to side. Perhaps more significant was the idea that the blood ebbed and flowed, tidelike, in the great vessels which were supposed to terminate in the nerves. It was against that sort of muddled intellectual background that Harvey enunciated and proved his great discovery.

He first observed that when an artery is cut, only blood escapes, and no air enters. Secondly, the blood escapes with force derived from contraction of the heart. Thirdly, that valves prevent return of the blood to either ventricle. Continuing, he wrote: "When I surveyed my mass of evidence I revolved in my mind what might be the quantity of blood that was transmitted...I began to wonder whether there might not be a motion in a circle as it were ..." [3.]

Harvey then showed that unless there was passage from the arteries to the veins, in the course of half an hour more blood would be ejected from the heart than could possibly be present in the whole body, and by ligaturing veins he showed that the blood in them was flowing toward the heart and therefore that blood enters a limb via the arteries and returns by the veins: "... it is absolutely necessary to conclude that the blood in the animal body is impelled in a circle and is in a state of endless motion; and that this is the action that the heart performs by means of its pulse ..." [4.]

That very abridged account summarises one of the greatest discoveries of pure science. Harvey's observations constitute the first *measurements* in any biological investigation. Its facts are carefully recorded; the observer conjectures a possible explanation; this hypothesis is tested and finds support from further observation; the work is repeatable by anyone having the technical skill to do so;

the conclusions are unambiguous. Harvey's discovery completely refuted some of the beliefs that were widely held up to that time.

Similar examples to Harvey's *De motu cordis* could be chosen from other branches of scientific knowledge. For instance, Newton's *Principia*; Faraday's *Researches;* Darwin's *Origin of Species*; etc. In many of the great scientific advances the original 'inspiration' of the scientist derives from the earlier work of someone else - as in the case of Fleming and Florey in the discovery of penicillin.

The advance of scientific knowledge is also closely related to improvement in technology. It was by his development of the telescope that Galileo was able to study astronomy; by his dexterity that Faraday demonstrated a variety of electrical phenomena, and the study of atomic structure by Thompson and Rutherford was dependent on sophisticated apparatus devised by numerous people of great ingenuity and skill.

Discoveries in this century have led to a remarkable change in the attempt to understand 'matter'. *The Quantum Theory* (Planck, 1901), *Relativity* (Einstein, 1905), and the *Uncertainty Principle* (Heisenberg, 1935), have abolished the 'picturability of the physical universe and no longer is there any confidence regarding the ultimate nature of 'matter'.

Sir James Frazer wrote in 1922: "The history of thought should warn us against concluding that the scientific theory of the world is necessarily complete and final. The generalisations of science are merely hypotheses devised to explain the ever shifting phantasmagoria which we dignify with the high-sounding names of the 'world' and the 'universe'." [5.]

Ideas about the nature of 'life' have also changed; the distinction between the living and the inanimate has become blurred. Advances in chemistry and biology have shown that human life has very much in common with simpler forms of animal life, and the new advances in physics and astronomy suggest that the fundamental structure of all matter is uncertain.

The value and importance of science derive from the experimental method of which Harvey's discovery is an excellent example. There are other realms of experience to which science is irrelevant; for instance; joy, beauty, wonder or worship. Science is restricted to a certain type of enquiry into *factual truth*. It is not concerned with meaning or purpose.

Sir William Osler, the greatest physician of his time, expressed this superbly in his address "The Leaven of Science" (1894): "Science has done much and will do more, to alleviate the unhappy condition in which so many of our fellow creatures live, and in no way more than in mitigating some of the horrors of disease; but we are too apt to forget that apart from, and beyond her domain lie those irresistible forces which alone sway the hearts of men. With Reason, Science never parts company, but with feeling, emotion, passion, what has she to do? They are not of her; they owe her no allegiance. She may study, analyse, and define, she can never control them, and by no means can their ways be justified to her." [6.]

What is the nature of Christian Belief?

This is more difficult to state succinctly than a statement about the methods of Science. Christianity is more than a matter of belief; it involves morality and behaviour; it is an attitude to life and it also involves discipleship. It cannot be the same today as it was one thousand years ago, and Christianity then was different from the Early Church, and will probably be different again in another thousand years, because at all times it relates to the different living predicament of each generation.

There has been an accretion of doctrines as generations have passed, without any apparent readiness on the part of the Church to discard outworn beliefs. What are the beliefs with which the great majority of Christians would agree, and which are also peculiar to Christianity? What do modern Christians believe that nobody else does?

The difficulty is that above all else, Christianity is the warming of the human heart toward an individual Person, Jesus Christ, regarding which, down the centuries, a massive superstructure of doctrine has built up. The extraordinary thing about this is that each generation has its men and women whose hearts warm to Jesus so that they regard Him as their *Lord,* and they attempt to live His Way. His Way - Agape - is all about Love - compassionate love for all mankind - and with this goes an inherent Trust that in some way this sort of attitude relates to the whole meaning and purpose of our existence. I am greatly impressed by this; I am convinced that it is true, all the more so as I become older.

Because this attitude of 'agape' is so difficult to

express in language or symbol, it has led to the formation of 'Christian Beliefs'; and more than is generally realised, the expression of these beliefs by one generation is liable to be misunderstood by a later generation, because they will often think differently and use a different style of language, both in speech and writing. As the former Bishop of Salisbury has said: "Christianity is about human life. It is not about religious devotions or practices, except in so far as these may help His people to see the Truth, and live their lives in the best possible way." (Rt. Rev. J. Austin Baker, inaugural sermon, 1982)

Our knowledge of Jesus derives from the Gospels, which are biased and partly contradictory! Yet the quality of Jesus Christ simply shines out through the contradictions of the New Testament, so that countless men and women have realised that He communicates insight to the reality of existence that is not to be found elsewhere.

It has been said that Christians should have avoided philosophic arguments about their beliefs in those early times; but that was never possible because it is of our human nature to state our experience about life in terms that satisfy our intellects. A pertinent question today is whether the doctrines that were developed and cherished by either the Early or the Medieval Church are clear and meaningful for our generation. The Gospels afford little or no support for many of the later theological assertions that have come to constitute much of Church doctrine. Certainly these do refer to genuine difficulties that have troubled Christians in the past, but should they still be retained and taught to our children and grandchildren as they stand? Can they be updated? Can any sort of agreement among Christians about this be achieved?

John Hick has posed this question in blunt terms: "It has become obvious that we are living at a turning point in the history of Christianity. This is because the development of modern Science has made much of the content of traditional Christian belief incredible ... The question today is whether such beliefs are of the permanent essence of Christianity, or whether they belong to the history of its interaction with the pre-scientific culture that has only recently come to an end." [7.]

This has become the most important theological question for our time.

Churchmen and Scientists.

Since the Reformation, there have been differences of outlook and much foolish writing about so-called antagonism between Science and Christianity, showing the reluctance of people who should have known better to accept and acknowledge change. Why should this be so? Religion and Science are two different aspects of mankind's quest for truth. Science seeks accurate factual knowledge, regardless of the consequences. Religion is concerned with truth about values and purposes in life, and relationships between God and man, both corporate and individual.

Hebrew perceptions in ancient Judaism, Greek perceptions in the thought of their ancient philosophers, have both contributed to the development of Christianity as it spread across Europe under protection of the Roman Empire. Later, religion seemed to conflict with the renaissance of learning, because, whereas Science leads to acceptance of new knowledge when this is proven, the discipline of Christianity is to sustain and uphold frail mankind by offering Authority to lean on in the human pilgrimage.

Fear is responsible for a large part of the difference between these two points of view. Science takes no cognizance of fear. Religion has confronted fear at every turn in mankind's long history, and from its very beginning, Christianity has always striven to overcome fear.

The execution of Giordano Bruno by the Inquisition in 1600 for propounding the Copernican hypothesis, the prohibition of Copernicus' and Kepler's books by the Vatican in 1615, and the enforced recantation by Galileo under the Inquisition in 1633, are well-known incidents that express mankind's fear of the new and unknown - all to the great discredit of the Church. Those tremendous discoveries by very great men indeed in no way contradicted or diminished Christianity, but they frightened the Church, which, feeling its Authority threatened, attempted to suppress new truth which it did not understand.

The fifty-five Founders of the Royal Society in 1660 are all believed to have been Christians (some maybe only nominally), but they were coming to perceive that by its intolerance the Church was becoming a barrier to scientific endeavour. Valid scientific discovery has been a fulfilment of truth and wonder that has seemed to many scientists a genuine religious experience. The discovery of a new, hitherto unrecognised fact (even a small contribution to the great pool of scientific knowledge) often confers a real sense of wonder and awe. (Archimedes is said to have been filled with joy when he shouted

'Eureka' on having a sudden inspiration about the truth of what has come to be known as the 'Archimedes Principle'.)

The Victorian era witnessed a stupendous advance in the sciences and their use in technology. It seems worthwhile to present this outpouring of scientific advances almost as a catalogue (NB. the dates following are taken from the *Encyclopaedia Britannica*):

About 1839 Daguerre and Fox Talbot pioneered photography; in 1840 Draper photographed the moon. Celluloid appeared in 1855 and Eastman photofilm in 1888. Petrol refining began in 1850 and oil-wells were drilled in Pennsylvania in 1859. Daimler produced his first motor-car in 1887 and Dunlop produced tyres in 1888.

The telegraph-printer in 1855, the transatlantic cable in 1858, the Bell telephone and the Remington typewriter in 1876, all began to change the previously accepted methods of communication.

Kelvin discovered absolute zero in 1848, and Dewar liquefied oxygen in 1891. Foucault measured the speed of light in 1849 and Michaelson and Morley's famous interferometer experiment in 1887 showed its peculiarity. Hertz described electro-magnetic waves in 1888 and Marconi demonstrated wireless telegraphy in 1889. Rontgen discovered X Rays in 1896.

Siemens developed the dynamo in 1867, and Westinghouse his brake system in 1872; electric welding arrived in 1877; Edison introduced electric lighting in 1879; the domestic gas fire followed in 1880. The steam turbine arrived in 1884 and the electric transformer in 1885. Robert Koch demonstrated the cause of tuberculosis in 1882.

Dresser produced aspirin in 1893, and Behring anti-tetanus serum in 1890.

Pasteur began his work on bacteria in 1858, Darwin published *The Origin of Species* in 1859, The Abbe Mendel stated the Laws of Heredity in 1865. Lister introduced antiseptic surgery, and Nobel introduced dynamite in 1867. Freud published *The Interpretation of Dreams* in 1900.

It really is no wonder that a great many people who did not understand scientific methods at all began to suppose that no knowledge could lie outside the realm of science. No wonder, too, that some Churchmen felt threatened.

Frederick Temple was Headmaster of Rugby School and edited *Essays and Reviews* published in 1861. In that book the future Archbishop wrote:"Physical Science, and a more thorough knowledge of the world, have enlarged our philosophy beyond the limits which bounded the Church of the Fathers. There are found to be more things in earth and heaven than were dreamt of in the Patristic theology. We can acknowledge the great value of the forms in which the first ages of the church defined the Truth, and yet refuse to be bound by them ..." [8.]

The aim of that book was to encourage discussion, it being known that many Churchmen were afraid to give offence by openly expressing their thoughts. Feelings ran high. The writers were accused of infidelity. The Bench of Bishops condemned them. Two Essayists were prosecuted in the Ecclesiastical Courts, and their sentences were only quashed on appeal to the Privy Council. The failure to realise the difference between Science and Christianity has been the greatest misfortune of the Church during the past two hundred years.

Indeed in *The Times* (Dec. 5th, 1984), the Bishop of Norwich, the Rt. Rev. M.A.P. Wood, wrote regarding embryo research: "Men and women of the broadest ethical and moral principles are beginning to realise that to open this Pandora's box of genetic engineering is to endanger the very basis of human and family life as we know it ... the government would be wise to put a moratorium on such experiments now."

Which government? Knowledge has never been constrained within national boundaries; it is - *per se* - amoral. Dynamite, nuclear power, pesticides and many other consequences of scientific research can be used by mankind for either good or evil purposes. And they are.

The Correct Relationship Between Christianity and Science.

Science and Religion are different aspects of mankind's endless quest toward Truth. Both seek a more profound understanding about Truth and Reality, God and Man. It has been said that Religion seeks the 'purpose' of living, and that Science seeks the 'power' to live. Indeed, man cannot live by bread alone - but without bread he cannot exist at all!

"I am the Way, the Truth, the Life" is a powerful dynamic call. Jesus is not saying: "Stay here, you know quite enough, just go on existing quietly." He is calling us to adopt His Way, to discover ever deeper truth; and that life lived fully is an exciting adventure. Curiosity is an innate attribute of humanity; which is only another way of saying that man is always seeking truth about reality.

Tennyson expressed this beautifully;

"Yet all experience is an arch wherethro',
        Gleams that untravelled world,
Whose margin fades for ever and for ever when I move.
        How dull it is to pause, to make an end,
To rest unburnished, not to shine in use.
        As tho' to breathe were life." [9.]

Perhaps this 'curiosity', this innate drive to search and find out, is ultimately the same urge that underlies the evolution of all life? The whole of material creation displays the same tendency to evolve and change. Why should there not be corresponding phenomena in the realm of religion? May not religion, too, be evolving? As mankind learns more 'religious technology', may he not gradually learn more and more about God? If prayer, worship, contemplation and ecstasy have any religious significance, then what about reading, writing, listening, thinking (meditation), constructive intelligent discussion? Surely these attributes also have religious value?

Teilhard de Chardin, the eminent Jesuit scientist and scholar, who died in 1955, has expressed this line of thought more clearly than anyone else. As a result of formulating such ideas he was forbidden by the Vatican in 1925 to publish any more. As an obedient Jesuit he submitted, but arranged through friends for his work to be published posthumously.

Teilhard de Chardin must have the last word: "Without doubt there is something which links the material and spiritual energy to make them a continuity. In the last resort there must be but one single energy in the world. If on the tree of life mammals are the dominant branch, then primates are its leading shoot, and in one clearly marked region at the centre, thought has been born. Abstract thought, logic, reasoned choice and invention, mathematics and art, the dreams and anxieties of love - all these activities of the inner life are simply the breaking forth of the new life-centre. Like Art, one might almost say, like Thought itself, Science at birth seemed but the product of an exuberant overflow of inward activity beyond the sphere of material necessities of life; but we who live in a world which it has revolutionised must acknowledge its social significance. Only Love can bring individuals to their perfect completion, because Love takes possession of them, and unites them with what lies deepest within them." [10.]

References.

1. Donald Hughes *Education* Rydal Press p.139

2. William Harvey *De motu cordis* (1628), quoted in *The Endless Quest* F.W.F. Westaway (Blackie), 1934, p.248-260

3. William Harvey, op. cit. p. 255

4. William Harvey, op. cit. p.259

5. J.G. Frazer *The Golden Bough* (MacMillan & Co) abb. Ed.1941 p.712

6. Wm Osler *Aequanimitas* (Lewis), 1948, p.93

7. John Hick *Christianity at the Centre*

8. F. Temple, *Essays and Reviews*, (1861)

9. Tennyson's poem Ulysses

10. Teilhard de Chardin 'Pensees' in *Hymn of the Universe* (Collins) 1965

Religion, Medicine and Healing

In primitive Society, religion and medicine were closely related. The high priest and the medicine man; the mystery of healing and the mystery of worship; fear of natural phenomena and the fear of death; the birth of babies and the annual rebirth of nature each springtime - all these things were connected and confused in primitive thought.

These early relationships of religion and medicine have been greatly clarified in this century by the work of psychologists, notably Freud, particularly in his book *Totem and Taboo*[1.] and also by anthropologists, notably Sir James Frazer in his book *The Golden Bough*. [2.] It is important to realise that this close relationship between medicine and religion certainly existed for several thousand years before the time of Jesus Christ.

Our concern is about the relationship of religion and medicine in much more recent times. First, though, two particular features about religion and medicine are important in the Teaching of Jesus Christ. Most people are familiar with some of the stories of healing in the Gospels: for instance, we read in St Matthew's Gospel, Chap. 4, 24: "... they brought him sick people that were taken with diverse diseases and torments, and those that were possessed with devils, and those which were lunatick, and those that had the palsy; and He healed them."

From this passage, (and there are many others like it in the Gospels), two very important conclusions seem to be inescapable. First, since there are many stories of Jesus healing people, it seems to me that our ordinary life-span is meant to be a healthy one. If I am wrong, then perhaps we should abolish not only the National Health Service, but also the professions of doctoring and nursing as well.

Secondly, Jesus' Healing Ministry utterly refutes the common belief of primitive mankind, viz that sickness and suffering are inflicted on us by God directly as a punishment for sin. Little Tommy doesn't catch measles because he was naughty at school, and God doesn't make Mrs Bloggs fall down the Church steps and break her leg because she hadn't put enough money into the collection!

Sickness and suffering are *not* inflicted on us individually by God as a punishment. I find it inconceivable that Jesus should deliberately ignore 'The Will of God' by going about healing people! The whole of that very primitive concept of sickness and suffering being God's punishment is demolished by the Gospel accounts of Jesus' Healing Ministry. I happen to suspect that this may be the essential Teaching that lies behind all the healing stories in the Gospels.

It is essential that Christian teachers should understand this fundamental aspect of Jesus Christ's Teaching. There are still plenty of Christian people who wear charms and amulets, who turn to primitive magic when they are unwell, or who ask, "Why has God done this to me?" *Fear* undoubtedly plays a very large part in this kind of thought and modern man is not so far removed from our primitive ancestors that we can afford to laugh at their beliefs.

A modern English physician, George Day, wrote in *The*

Lancet some years ago: "The vast majority of ills in man or beast leave the body with no permanent disability; but in Man they can often cripple the mind or spirit. The commonest and most disabling complication of any human ailment is *'fear'*, fear engendered by ignorance, misapprehension, or belief in things that are no longer true."

Modern Scientific Medicine.

Today, medical knowledge has changed so much that we just cannot think of illness and disease as people did two thousand years ago in terms of torments, devils, lunatick and palsy. Our problem today is how to relate the marvellous modern advances in medicine to our understanding of Christian teaching and the way of life that Jesus taught.

Many medical and surgical conditions are essentially mechanical: many lumps and blemishes can be surgically removed; fractures can often be pinned or plastered; painful joints and a variety of other things can now be removed or even replaced. These are the sort of things that a motor-car 'suffers' when it breaks a spring or needs a new tyre!

There are other diseases that come about because the machinery is, so to speak, "creaking a bit and needing greasing" and which with our present-day knowledge we can sometimes relieve. For instance there is now a range of antibiotics for very many different infections, there is insulin for diabetes, vitamins for rickets or scurvy, or iron for anaemia...the list grows and grows every year. Our generation has lived through an amazing period of discovery and advance in medicine and surgery.

Then, too, there are some illnesses that we have learned to prevent: for instance, thanks to clever engineers, dysentery and cholera can be eliminated by the purification of food and water supplies; and due to the efforts of clever scientists there are various immunization procedures against, for example, whooping cough, typhoid fever or tuberculosis.

I do not find any directly religious or Christian aspect in the sort of conditions that I have so far referred to - except to observe that, whereas some people in the rich countries of the world can afford to have these amenities, our brethren in the poorer countries usually cannot. Consequently, some two thousand millions of these poorer people - men, women and children - do not have the safe drinking water and sanitation that could immediately eliminate thirty per cent of disease prevalent in the developing countries. [3.]

All the diseases I have so far referred to constitute the bulk of those life-threatening illnesses which have become so much better controlled thanks to the tremendous advances in medical knowledge during the past hundred years or so. This better care is the result of the impact and power of science to improve the physical standards of our lives. I do not see this as having anything to do directly with the *purpose* of our lives.

What is the doctor for?

However, many of our modern illnesses relate directly to contemporary bad habits and lack of personal discipline: for instance, over-eating, excessive alcohol, tobacco smoking and many road accidents. One should probably add venereal diseases to this list. Is it any less promiscuous to drive a car under the influence of alcohol, than it is to contract AIDS? Is smoking or over-eating a responsible way to use money?

What, them, is the purpose of medicine, by which I mean, what is the modern doctor for? All the highly sophisticated and scientific techniques used in medicine today can only examine the structure and function of either our anatomical parts or our physiological systems; none of them can evaluate the whole person. Not one of our marvellous scientific resources will disclose that common disabling complication of illness that George Day referred to as *fear!*

Undoubtedly, an essential part of the doctor's task is to evaluate the *whole person*. If you take all the severe injuries, all the cancer, heart attacks and strokes, these are certainly outnumbered in our western civilisation by the "minor" ill-health associated with *loneliness, selfishness, guilt and fear* - and modern scientific medicine is not equipped (nor is it appropriate) to deal with any of these, and I suspect it never will be.

Many people today are 'ill' because they or their loved ones have got their values in life all messed up. Their problems are due, for instance, to divorce, abortion, greed or debt. There are all the secret sorrows, secret fears, secret guilt. Or perhaps they have no one to love, or no one to be loved by. Very many people today are confused as to the purpose of their lives; and this has nothing to do with the science of medicine.

Of course many such people "go to tell their doctor" but the story he or she then hears is so often about headaches, backache, tiredness or indigestion, etc. and so because doctors are only human, and because of our human frailty, the story is often cut short with a pen and a prescription pad. The average GP in England today issues about three hundred prescriptions each week. The modern doctor's training does not necessarily make him a good pastor, a good confessor, or even a good friend! Nor does the clergyman's theological training necessarily make him a good pastor, a good confessor, or a good friend!

Opportunity for the Church?

Consider these four observations: The philosopher Bertrand Russell, an atheist, wrote in 1932: "There are certain things our age needs, and the root of the matter is that it needs Christian Love and Compassion. If you feel this you have a motive for existence, a reason for Courage." [4.]

Carl Gustav Jung, the great Swiss psychiatrist, wrote in 1930: "In my medical experience, as well as in my own life, I have again and again been faced with the mystery of Love, and have never been able to explain it; Man can try to name Love, but if he has even a grain of wisdom he will lay down his arms and call it - GOD." [5.]

John Wesley, priest of the Church of England, wrote in 1747: "The Love of God effectually prevents all the bodily disorders that the passions produce; it becomes the most powerful of all the means of health and long life." [6.]

Quite a long time ago St John wrote: "Perfect Love

casteth out Fear."

But there are also guilt and forgiveness, two more "opposites" which, like fear and love, are surely the Church's concern?

Today the Christian Church has an enormous opportunity for leadership because the medical profession has not yet come to terms with the ethical consequences of the rapid scientific advances already mentioned, and there is increasing public concern about the moral dilemmas that arise as a result. These moral uncertainties will increase in the foreseeable future, for we have now entered the era of test-tube babies, and the increased understanding of the genetic code is already raising a host of new dilemmas.

The significance of the twentieth century population explosion is as yet hardly realised, but doctors already have to decide priorities for hospital admission, and to balance the life prospects of a defective baby against the family stresses of rearing such a child. I find it helps to remember that a new *person* only begins its human life when an infant takes its first independent breath.[7, 8.]

There is increasing emphasis on the "Sanctity of Life" these days. One can deplore abortion, and the prospect of legalising voluntary euthanasia, but the concept of the Sanctity of Physical Life is an ethic derived from very ancient pre-Christian society long ago. It was associated with a primitive belief that the indefinite continuation of physical life was normal, and that death only occurred by reason of accident, magic, or the intervention of the gods.

The Church Assembly's Board of Social Responsibility, a very responsible body of Christian opinion, made this declaration in 1965, and it deserves far more public attention than it has yet received: "Nursing, medicine and surgery are the response of society to human sickness. To call the object of that need, and the response 'preservation of *life* is misleading'. What a patient needs is care and relief. In the second place, he wants restoration of health, or the nearest return to normal that can be achieved. Since preserving his *life* is a *sine qua non* of restoring his health, it is an end which those who have care of him pursue, and ought to pursue, *but it is not in itself an ultimate*." [9]

Physically, there is a time to live and a time to die. It is the Spiritual and Personal life of people that is important, not merely the length of their physical existence. It seems to be part of our human predicament that there is no way that we can opt out of suffering and anguish on our journey through life. Diseases change and the resources of medicine for treating them also change, as scientific knowledge advances; but human anxiety, fear, grief and misery remain with us just the same. They are part of our human condition and in a Christian context, they cannot be ignored.

In considering sickness and healing from a Christian point of view, we must not seek primitive magic. The teaching of Jesus Christ opposes this. Do not expect healing by supernatural intervention - God doesn't work that way. There is no point in quibbling about the rituals which the church has practised down the centuries and which may comfort some people today; but always remember that these are only one aspect, only one minor part, of the whole healing ministry to better the health of all God's people.

Much sickness is not a maladjustment of the physical body to its physical environment, but rather a maladjustment of the human mind and spirit to reality, to God. If we can live with our own values aright, then we will be able to pass on something of the Love of God to our fellow-men and help others to discover what they are *LIVING FOR* - which is to find their own *SALVATION.*

References.

1. Freud S *Totem and Taboo* Pelican, 1938

2. Fraser J.G *The Golden Bough* MacMillan, (abb. Ed.) 1941

3. Brit. med. J. 1992, 304, 190

4. Russell, Bertrand *Impact of Science on Society* Allan and Unwin, 1952 (quoted in C.A. Coulson, *"Science and Christian Belief"*, OUP, 1955, p.111)

5. Jung, C.G. (quoted in C.A. Coulson *Science and Christian Belief* OUP, 1955, p.110)

6. Wesley J Primitive Physic (introduction), 1747

7. Genesis, Chap. 2

8. Eden and Holland Manual of Obstetrics Churchill, 1940

9. Board of Social Responsibility of the Church Assembly: "Decisions about life and death", a problem in modern medicine: Ch. 111, p.24, C.I.O. 1965